Unbuilt Calgary

UNBUILT CALGARY

Stephanie White

DUNDURN
TORONTO

Copyright © Stephanie White, 2012

All rights reserved. No part of this publication may be reproduced, stored in a retrieval system, or transmitted in any form or by any means, electronic, mechanical, photocopying, recording, or otherwise (except for brief passages for purposes of review) without the prior permission of Dundurn Press. Permission to photocopy should be requested from Access Copyright.

Project Editor: Michael Carroll
Editor: Matt Baker
Design: Courtney Horner
Printer: Friesens

Library and Archives Canada Cataloguing in Publication

White, Stephanie, 1949-
    Unbuilt Calgary / Stephanie White.

Issued also in electronic formats.
ISBN 978-1-4597-0330-8

    1. Calgary (Alta.)--History. 2. Calgary (Alta.)--Buildings, structures, etc.--History. 3. City planning--Alberta--Calgary--History. I. Title.

FC3697.3.W55 2012   971.23'38   C2012-903224-7

1 2 3 4 5   16 15 14 13 12

We acknowledge the support of the **Canada Council for the Arts** and the **Ontario Arts Council** for our publishing program. We also acknowledge the financial support of the **Government of Canada** through the **Canada Book Fund** and **Livres Canada Books**, and the **Government of Ontario** through the **Ontario Book Publishing Tax Credit** and the **Ontario Media Development Corporation**.

Care has been taken to trace the ownership of copyright material used in this book. The author and the publisher welcome any information enabling them to rectify any references or credits in subsequent editions.

J. Kirk Howard, President

Printed and bound in Canada.

VISIT US AT
Dundurn.com | Definingcanada.ca | @dundurnpress | Facebook.com/dundurnpress

Dundurn
3 Church Street, Suite 500
Toronto, Ontario, Canada
M5E 1M2

Gazelle Book Services Limited
White Cross Mills
High Town, Lancaster, England
LA1 4XS

Dundurn
2250 Military Road
Tonawanda, NY
U.S.A. 14150

Table of Contents

Preface   9

Introduction   11

The CPR Landscape

1. Canadian Pacific Railway   17
2. CPR Gardens   19
3. The Shape of Calgary   21
4. Transportation-Driven Planning   25
5. The Promotion of Calgary   30
6. Seattle World's Fair and the Calgary Tower: The Regional Context   36

Downtown

7. Introduction   41
8. The Thomas Mawson Plan for Calgary   43
9. Traffic and Parking   46
10. The Calgary Civic Centre   50

11. Relocation of VIA Rail Terminal	57
12. Calgary Municipal Building Competition	61

Roads and Bridges

13. South Bow River Parkway	71
14. Centre Street Bridge	75
15. St. Patrick's Island Bridge	79
16. Fish Creek LRT Bridge	82

Oil and Gas Urbanism

17. The Clipping Files	89
18. 1960s Downtown Office Boom	91
19. 9th Avenue and 4th Street Southwest	93
20. Downtown Roads	96
21. 7th Avenue	100

Outside the Downtown Core

22. The 1910 Aerial Drawing	107
23. University of Calgary	109
1958 Plan	110
Long-Range Development Plan	112
24. Shouldice/Montgomery	114
25. River's Edge Village	117
26. Olympic Arches	121
27. Happy Valley	123
28. Sarcee Motor Hotel	128

Housing

    29. Wheat Boom Subdivisions   135

    30. Communities on Lakes   140

    31. Escarpments   143

        St. Andrew's Heights   144

        Regal Terrace   148

    32. Hills   150

        Earth-Sheltered Housing   150

        Four Square House and Subdivision   153

Geology and Metaphor

    33. Geology and Geography   159

Neighbourhoods

    34. Calgary's Quadrants   165

    35. Mawson/Manchester   170

        Mawson, 1912   170

        The Manchester Area Redevelopment Plan   172

    36. Inner-City Neighbourhood Main Streets   175

        Mission   177

        Inglewood   178

Housing and Densification

    37. Densification   183

        The Beltline   184

    38. Laneway Houses   187

    39. The Scale of Houses Between 1955 and 1975   191

STAMPEDE GROUNDS

   40. The Stampede in a Regional Context   199

   41. Stampede Accessibility   203

       Mawson   205

       Chandler Kennedy Analysis   205

EAST VILLAGE

   42. Cantos Music Foundation and the King Edward Hotel   211

   43. East Village Plans   215

       2005 East Village Area Redevelopment Proposal   216

       2007 Rivers District Community Revitalization Plan   217

       East Village, Rivers District, Riverwalk   220

Bibliography   223

Index   226

Preface

Writing this book has been an interesting process. It isn't the book I started out to write, but as it developed, the importance of land and landscape came to the fore in what is often considered to be a very tough city. I have become aware of the distance between underlying values and public relations. What impressed me is how many ideas are still being developed today that appeared in plans made at Calgary's very beginning.

Both sides of my family came to Calgary during the wheat boom as British immigrants; my mother's grandfather was busy flinging together small houses in Albert Park in 1909, just at the end of the wheat boom and its associated real estate bubble. Another grandfather surveyed the layout of the Stampede racetrack on his honeymoon in 1907. As children, both my parents lived on the same street, 18A Southwest, on the edge of the city — beyond was prairie and buffalo wallows, and the endless summers of the Depression.

I worked in Calgary during the architectural boom in the late 1970s and early 1980s; like so many after it crashed, I left to find work elsewhere. One can be most nostalgic about Calgary and the landscapes of southern Alberta when one no longer lives in it, so much so that I eventually wrote a doctoral dissertation about how modernism in architecture and planning hit the landscapes of Calgary, and how Calgary bent it to fit.

It is repeated several times throughout the text about how easily unbuilt projects were discarded — the drawings and all the accompanying files. The architects are long gone, and there is no one to ask anymore. However, those drawings that were found — ink and pencil on paper — can be terrifically eloquent, and so we must thank the generations of draftsmen, designers, and architects who had so many ideas about how to live well, and how to live well in the city.

Linda Fraser, of the Canadian Architectural Archives at the University of Calgary, has been extraordinarily helpful, as have Lindsay Moir of the Glenbow Museum Archives; Iris Morgan of the Maps, Academic Data, Geographic Information Centre at the University of Calgary; and Carolyn Ryder of the Community Archives of the Calgary Public Library.

Tom Martin, Gerald Forseth, Dan Jenkins, Manfred Grote, Karl Pokorny, Ali Famili, Barry Johns, Bob Ellsworthy, Rick Balbi, David Lachapelle, and Darrel Babuk all took the time to discuss Calgary and their work in it, and to them I am very grateful. Not all the projects I looked at have been included, but they were all thought about and their circumstances and ideas incorporated somewhere in the text, even if not by name.

I would like to acknowledge the support of the Canada Council for the Arts and its Alberta Creative Development Initiative program for the research portion of this project.

Introduction

Calgary has long been known as a typical boom/bust town: its mayors have been boosters and caretakers, it grows in spurts and then lies fallow, it explodes and crashes. But, as a city, Calgary is never dismayed by its slow periods; it plans, always plans for its next glorious future. Because growth is not steady, many of these plans aren't implemented in their entirety — fragments are built, and partial plans are rushed into production before the next downturn, which always comes sooner than anyone predicts. By the next boom, these plans are out-of-date relics of a previous era.

In these superseded plans are visions for Calgary that tell much about the social history of this place, its ambitions, its particularly maverick behaviour, and its opacity to the rest of Canada. The projects in this book are ones that were particularly prescient and contain ideas still in play today. What is surprising about many is how long ago these ideas were formed.

Calgary started as a fort in 1875, became a CPR service depot in 1883, and by time the 1901–13 wheat boom crashed, Calgary had established itself as a centre for settlement.

Here are three telling images to start this book of Calgary visions. The Dominion Survey Map of 1884 documents homestead plots and the new railway; this is what was actually, measurably, here. The next is an 1885 photograph of what Calgary looked like. The bottom image is a declarative CPR plan of downtown Calgary in 1884 drawn up to attract both investors and commercial development by implying there was more building already in progress than there actually was.

This book also describes Calgary in various contexts larger than the city itself, which is sometimes self-absorbed to the point that things such as recessions, international political events, and federal and provincial changes are taken personally. For many architects whose

[12] UNBUILT CALGARY

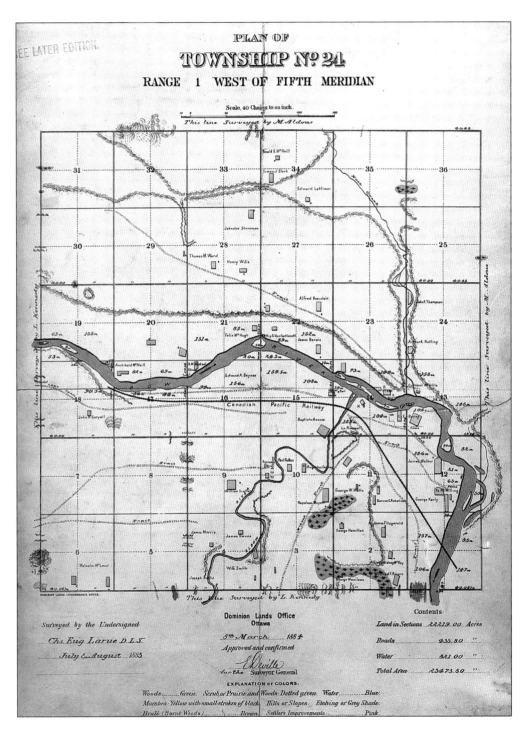

Figure 0-1. Surveyed by Charles Eugene Larue, July 3, 1883, and approved March 8, 1884, this is the actual Dominion Lands Office survey based on the Dominion Grid of townships and ranges. Township 24: six miles by six miles, divided into 36,640-acre sections. The marshy spot between sections 35 and 36 is in Albert Park today; the marsh straddling the corners of sections 2, 3, 10, and 11 is where Mawson planned his artisans' village and where Manchester stands today. The lighter squares are cleared land, a condition of the Homestead Act, and the tiny black dots nearby are houses. The CPR line doesn't go much farther than today's downtown core.
Glenbow Archives NA-3487-9.

Figure 0-2. This 1885 photograph shows Calgary as a string of hostelries, hotels, small houses and storefronts, and a couple of churches, all facing south to the CPR tracks. Calgary has become such a green city; here, there is not a tree in sight. As none of these buildings are indicated on the Dominion Survey done in July 1883, and the plots only registered in January 1884, these buildings were all built in a year.

Glenbow Archives NA-4035-77.

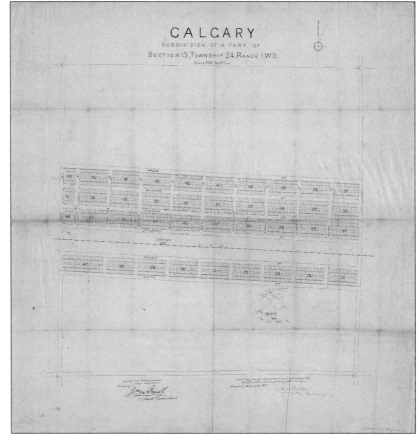

Figure 0-3. This 1884 CPR Land Department map is signed by A.W. McVittie, surveyor, and states, "This Plan is correct and is prepared under the provisions of the North West Territories Registration of Titles Ordinance. Winnipeg, January 1st 1884." The avenues are named after CPR financiers, presidents, and executives: Smith (11th Avenue), Stephen for 8th, McIntyre for 7th. Atlantic and Pacific Avenues flank the tracks, tying Calgary into a national landscape.

Glenbow Archives G3504-C151-1884-C212.

particular projects were not built, the circumstances are as vivid today as they were thirty years ago. It is time to step back and look at some of these unbuilt projects as significant declarations of the intent to build a responsive and thoughtful city. A factor in Calgary's development has been its relatively transient population. Many Canadians have spent a few years in Calgary, especially during its boom times, and then moved on. Too, the young average age of Calgarians indicates that not everyone stays after they retire — the Okanagan and Vancouver Island beckon. So, while the population steadily increases, there are not a lot of people, or families, who have seen the city through all its phases. People are transferred to Calgary, or come to Calgary on spec, single or with young families, and take the city much as they find it. Its past is not their past, and they share Calgary's present but not necessarily its future.

A Laurie Anderson quotation on the hoardings outside the Performing Arts Centre when it was undergoing renovation in 2012 said something along the lines of the more we tell our stories, the more they are no longer ours, meaning that we release our stories into the world. It can also mean that stories told and retold — as is often the case in Calgary, which has a well-trodden narrative — cease to be our own real experiences. The stories here revolve around a number of quite untold architectural and planning proposals, and several over-told plans that perhaps need to be told slant. Hopefully, this book will join the shelf of previous books about the shape of Calgary that collectively make sense of this city.

THE CPR LANDSCAPE

Chapter 1

Canadian Pacific Railway

The Canadian Pacific Railway received 500,000 acres and $500,000 for the building of a trans-Canada rail link, a condition of British Columbia entering Confederation in 1873. The railway was preceded by the Dominion Land Survey, which applied a six-mile square grid from Winnipeg, the first meridian, to the Rocky Mountains. Calgary is on the fifth meridian. A half section west is Centre Street and the site of the CPR station, which in 1967, for Centennial year, was replaced by the Husky Tower, now the Calgary Tower. The CPR station went underground, disappearing from public view, a reflection of how, by the 1960s, the oil-and-gas landscape had started to obliterate the older CPR urban structure.

Calgary is one of a series of cities shaped by the CPR, which include Winnipeg, Regina, and Vancouver. The same grid, the same relationship between commercial zoning and the train station, and the same social determinism in the setting out of districts for CPR managers and CPR workers characterize early CPR urbanism. The placement of the rail yards condemned some sectors to be forever industrial and worker housing. Other areas, for Hudson's Bay Company factors and CPR brass, remain exclusive housing districts today.

This commercial map indicates a density of downtown development that competes with contemporary images of stores on 8th and 9th Avenues that show a very low density: no building touches another, the streets are broad and empty. The downtown core has been a gradual filling in of this original urban diagram to achieve a density forecast at Calgary's very beginning.

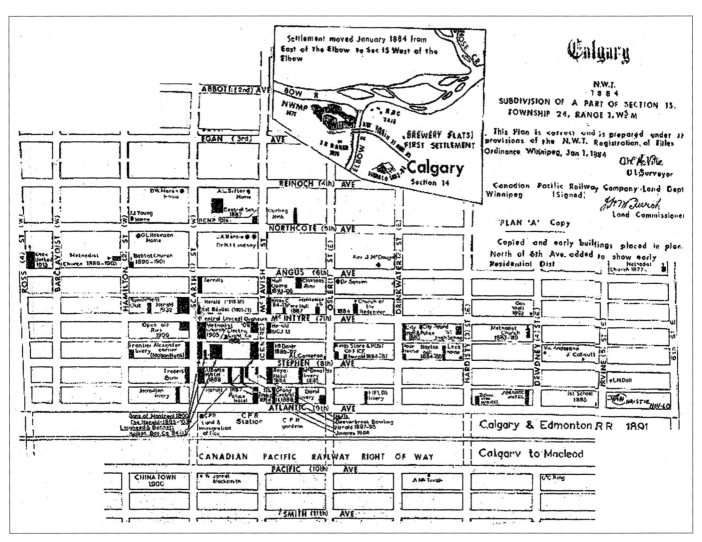

Figure 1-1. This is perhaps confusing: the downtown area is laid out in blocks, possibly from the McVittie drawing, but amended in 1960 by Ian Christie, showing "early buildings placed in plan. North of 6th Avenue added to show early Residential District." 1960 was the beginning of the dismantling of old downtown Calgary as the oil-and-gas boom started to bite into it. This is one of the first indications that there was an old and a new Calgary. In Calgary of 1900, Chinatown was on 10th Avenue between 1st and 2nd Streets Southwest, and an open air rink sat on 7th Avenue and 1st Street West. In 1892 a gas well was on the corner of 7th Avenue and 4th Street East.
Community and Historical Resources, Calgary Public Library.

Chapter 2

CPR Gardens

One cannot overestimate the importance of the CPR to western Canada. A hundred and forty years later, in the light of energy security and sustainability, the benefit of rail over roads is being reconsidered. In the discussion of unbuilt projects for Calgary, we could include no-longer built projects that exist only in photographs or drawings and that, if considered today, would set Calgary off in a new direction. One such project is the block east of the CPR station that, until the 1930s, was taken up by a large market garden. Photographs show beds of cabbages, beans, and potatoes, bordered with pinks and marigolds, and gravelled paths lined with young fruit trees. Today, it reminds one of the *agriponicos* of Cuba, where fruit and vegetable production now covers almost all open space in Cuba's cities, including the grounds of disused factories, parks, and parking lots, producing several million tons of food per year. This is food security, and it is as important in the twenty-first century as energy and water security.

Were the CPR gardens simply demonstration projects, or did they provide food for the railway? One suspects the latter, with surplus distributed amongst CPR employees. This was an urban landscape before the industrialization of food supply, and because of that it offers a template for a more sustainable future. An ongoing debate about Calgary's steady expansion into surrounding farmland concerns the displacement of agriculture in favour of low-density housing development. It is possible that allotments, very much in favour in inner-city communities such as Hillhurst and Inglewood, might reinstate intense local food production, such as that seen with Vancouver's 2003 Food Action Plan for rooftop gardens, community gardens, farmers' markets, coordinated food processing, and distribution facilities for low-income citizens. The surprise was to find that this was a reality initiated by what was then corporate Calgary, a century ago.

Figure 2-1. These are the gardens to the east of the CPR station, on 9th Avenue. Vegetable plots are set out in formal parterres edged by flowering borders. We take for granted the provisioning of passenger trains, not thinking that in the 1890s food would have been gathered along the route, non-perishables warehoused, fresh meat and stored vegetables — or in-season fresh fruit and vegetables — picked up at each station. Pat Burns provisioned the Grand Trunk Pacific Railway as it was being built, and this was the basis of his fortune.
Topley Studio / Library and Archives Canada / PA-026186.

Chapter 3

The Shape of Calgary

There is a taxonomy of cities based on their origins: company towns have few civic spaces, as they are not based on demonstrations of democracy but on corporate organization — there is work and there is where the workers live. Usually, such towns remain small, their size dependent upon the technology and labour force needed to maintain the industry. Other cities, such as Halifax, originated as military camps. Laid out and occupied by the British Army in 1754, at Halifax's heart is a parade square dominated by an Anglican church at its east end and surrounded by a series of small city blocks that were originally barracks. Halifax is still a military town, and although the Citadel is a famous tourist site, it is also Department of National Defence property. The Grand Parade is Halifax's potent and ceremonial civic space, more so than the lawn in front of the provincial courthouse or the legislature.

On the other hand, both Edmonton and Calgary started as forts, which exist today as historic reconstruction, their sense of civic engagement sidelined to a historical curiosity, part of a deep history of little relevance compared to subsequent civic definitions. This is quite clear in Calgary: historically the conjunction of the Elbow and the Bow Rivers was an aboriginal meeting place. So many of our Canadian cities and towns started at such meeting sites, whether it be a small river meeting a large one, such as all the towns along the South Saskatchewan or the Fraser or the Mackenzie Rivers; or a river meeting a lake, as seen in any of the cities and towns on the Great Lakes; or a river meeting the ocean, in places such as Vancouver and Bella Coola. Settlement needs fresh water. Forts went where native settlements or meeting places had been because of the presence of fresh water, and the remains of forts are generally somewhere at the heart of all Canadian cities.

In Calgary the 1875 North-West Mounted Police fort at the corner of the Elbow and Bow Rivers protected First Nations from the predations of the American whiskey industry, which was making incursions into what was then the Northwest Territories, a generally unpoliced and unsettled area. Its southern boundary, unrecognized by both the Blackfoot and itinerant traders, had been established as the 49th parallel by the Jay Treaty of 1794. The purpose of the NWMP was twofold: to maintain a good relationship with indigenous peoples in the British territories and to maintain British sovereignty in the face of the manifest destiny of the United States. As First Nations compliance was necessary and even vital, forts were placed where those First Nations already had long-established bases.

When the prairies were surveyed by the Dominion Land Survey in the 1870s and 1880s, for both the route of the CPR and the preparatory division of land for settlement that the railway would enable, the location of the forts influenced the route of the railway. The linkage between military use and transportation systems is informative. During the Riel Rebellion of 1885, the NWMP travelled by CPR train from Winnipeg to Duck Lake — a trip of a couple of days rather than the two weeks it would take by horse. The quashing of the Riel Rebellion was facilitated by the CPR, a transportation system, and the linking of all the southern prairie forts by the railway and the telegraph meant that military response could be almost instantaneous. The ancient space-time continuum of the indigenous landscape was irreversibly changed by the coming of the rail.

Although Fort Calgary was the important beginning of the city, the Canadian Pacific Railway set up a rival centre based not on military order but on company influence. In CPR towns the potent site of power was the CPR station. Because the NWMP was not a military force at the scale of the British Army in Halifax or Victoria, and was just a police force meant to keep local aboriginal groups onside and to protect CPR interests, downtown Calgary developed an urban landscape of power that radiated out from the CPR station. The station was on 9th Avenue, and next to it was the CPR hotel, the Palliser. Across the intersection was the Grain Exchange, and across 9th from that was the Robin Hood Flour Mills, a significant landmark which stood until 1975. A block away from the Grain Exchange was the Hudson's Bay Company (HBC) store, the particular terracotta design of which was based on Harrods, the famous department store in London that had opened in 1898. Across 1st street was the Bank of Montreal, the bank of the CPR and the Hudson's Bay. This was Calgary's component of the extended landscape of Scottish Montreal. Both the Canadian Pacific Railway and the Hudson's Bay Company were populated by Scots. Lord Strathcona, for example, who turned the North-West Mounted Police into Lord Strathcona's Horse, a regiment raised in Calgary for the Boer War, was Donald Smith, the financier of the Canadian Pacific and the official who pounded in the last spike at Craigellachie, British Columbia. Both the CPR and the Hudson's Bay had Canadian headquarters in Montreal. Calgary was a link in the chain of commerce and influence that stretched from London to the Far East.

Between 1880 and 1900, Calgary existed as a company town, and the company was the Canadian Pacific Railway. Notice there was no dominating church or military presence, and City Hall was a couple of blocks away, in what was, at the time, a relatively insignificant location across the street from the market. Changes in transportation after the Second World War, such as the emergence of commercial air travel, an increase in car ownership, coordination with the U.S. trucking industry, and the building of both the Interstate Highway System and the Trans-Canada

Highway, diminished the importance of the public rail services, and with that diminution came the loss of the importance of the train station. In the 1960s, passenger service was severely curtailed, and by the late 1960s, the CPR separated various branches of its operations — freight, hotels, real estate, express services, its airline CP Air, and its extensive telecommunications network — and sold most of its subsidiaries off over the next twenty years.

Unlike Winnipeg and Vancouver, both of which had huge stone neo-classical railway stations for both the CPR and the CNR, Calgary had a long, low, linear platform station. Calgary in its early days wasn't a big player in the overall CPR network; it was really just a stop between Winnipeg and Vancouver and the link to the provincial capital in Edmonton, which was served by the Grand Trunk and Pacific Railway, later the CNR.

Figure 3-1. The front of the CPR Station on 9th Avenue. The Palliser is on the right edge of the photograph. This is an example of a busy and vital corporate urban open space, rather than a civic space such as those found in front of city halls or public parks. The forecourt to the railway station is largely used for parking and deliveries. Railway stations are double-fronted: one side faces the city and the other is the platform facing the train, where emotional welcomes and farewells are held. This street front is not emotional. It is a service space, although probably one of the largest formal open areas in the city at the time.
University of Saskatchewan Archives, Keith Ewart Photograph Collection, Railway Stations.

When, in the early 1960s, Canada's centennial appeared on the new horizon of national identity, many cities felt that they must come up with major centennial projects by 1967 to mark the new postwar Canada, to attract tourists travelling the country in ever-increasing numbers, and, in the process, to brand their cities. Projects such as the Sudbury Nickel or the Wawa Goose, and many other celebratory markers of cities across Canada, often have their origins in a centennial project. For its part, Calgary built the Husky Tower on 9th Avenue and Centre Street, replacing the old Canadian Pacific Railway station, which was relocated underneath a shopping centre and office complex, Palliser Square, built by the CPR beside the Palliser Hotel.

However, just before this act of erasure, in 1962 the Canadian Pacific Railway hired a New York planning firm to replan their land holdings on the south side of 9th Avenue between 1st Street East and 1st Street West. At the same time, the City of Calgary commissioned the Robinson Hanson Report and the 1960 Transportation Plan, which recommended the removal of the barrier that the CPR railway tracks presented to southward downtown expansion. The CPR main line, and the CPR ownership of the block-wide swath through downtown Calgary, was like a river with a couple of bridges across it: downtown was effectively an island surrounded by the Bow River on the north and west edges, the Elbow River on the east and the CPR tracks on the south. One recommendation was to relocate the tracks to the south bank of the Bow River and allow the downtown to then flood south. This was an era when rivers and lakefronts were seen as barriers rather than amenities and were thus suitable for transportation corridors. A well-known and notorious example of this attitude underpins the Gardiner Expressway in Toronto, which, among other things, separates downtown Toronto from the shore of Lake Ontario. By 1960 the site of Fort Calgary, long gone, had become a Canadian National Railway terminal yard forming the industrial east end of downtown, bordered by two rivers and the tracks. With the removal of CNR activities, the land could easily become a freeway interchange. In the early 1960s, it was inevitable that transportation led planning, an ethos that sank deep into many cities, the results of which we still live with.

Chapter 4

Transportation-Driven Planning

With the presentation of a possible strategy for the development of CPR's land holdings on 9th Avenue (they weren't planning to leave their valuable, centralized site, no matter what the City of Calgary was thinking of), Gordon Atkins, a newly graduated twenty-five-year-old architect who had set up his own firm in 1962, reacted violently to these proposals. His alternative proposals occupy an enormous file of drawings in the Canadian Architectural Archives, including his design for the June 1963 cover of *Maclean's* magazine on this topic, the re-imagining of Calgary. The CPR had hired a New York planner, R. Dowling, who proposed a plan for a whizzy, spaceship sort of figure to mark the location of the new station, something with the formal placemaking power of the Guggenheim Museum in New York, finished just five years earlier — Atkins was particularly vehement about this proposal:

These sketches show, in elevation, the transportation center centre as proposed by CPR's planning consultant (R. Dowling of New York). The conglomeration of buildings is multi-directional, multi-functional, and so lacking in any statement of function or clear-cut unified expression that they become cartoonish and obvious.

That Atkins also protested the proposed removal of the barrier to southward development that was, and still is, the CPR main line had much to do with his personal background. He had grown up in southern Alberta, in Cardston, a Mormon town connected to the United States border and Utah by the Alberta Railway and Irrigation Company (later acquired by the CPR). Mormons had developed irrigation technology in Utah and were invited to settle 500,000 acres on the St. Mary

River in southern Alberta in exchange for building an irrigation canal system, which was duly completed in 1900. The Waterways Treaty of 1909 divided the waters of the St. Mary and the Milk Rivers, and continues to plague southern Alberta to this day.[1]

Gordon Atkins understood dry land and the importance of railways and compact grid cities with tight borders, of which Cardston was one. He also had a new postwar American education (the University of Washington in Seattle), in which transportation planning figured largely, dominated by the influence of the American planner Robert Moses, who had advocated the channelling of traffic into parkways, tunnels, and interchanges since the 1930s. The major postwar adjustment in urban and suburban transportation policy was a shift from parkways, literally limited-access roads flanked by forest, to large concrete freeways hurling suburban commuters into downtown cores. Freeways into the centres of cities had become postwar planning orthodoxy, no doubt much debated in architecture and planning schools in the 1950s. Gordon Atkins was ten years younger than the Philadelphia architect and theorist Robert Venturi and started his practice just as Venturi's 1961 book, *Complexity and Contradiction in Architecture*, was published: change was coming fast, and a young, smart architect such as Gordon Atkins would have been bursting with ideas about the complexity of making responsive and responsible urban places rather than generalized, often abstract, transportation and zoning models.

Atkins's key drawing is of the little island that is still downtown Calgary, a tiny grid bounded on all sides that displays the potent, historic civic pattern of Calgary. To break down the barriers and allow the commercial office core to diffuse would have destroyed this heart.

As a direct critique of the 1963 City of Calgary's proposed freeway into the downtown, necessitated by suburban neighbourhoods gobbling up farmland all around the edges of the city, Atkins proposed that 7th Avenue become a transportation corridor that put both local and regional buses, a streetcar/light rail system, the continental railway line, taxis, and bicycle lanes all in a carefully stacked section. Cars were notably absent in this proposal — it was all public transit, and without surface parking lots that still dominate the downtown core, there was lots of room for vertical expansion. What is surprising is how prescient Atkins was and how strong was his vision of a centralized, compact city that used public transit to keep its edges close. A sense of proximity at many scales is evident in the drawings: one should be able to look out of an office window and see someone at a bus stop, while a taxi goes by, and underneath is the rumble of the transcontinental train, overhead, a helicopter — it is a kind of gentle, small-town, high-modern vision of verticality.

Because everything is in its place in Atkins's proposal, and there are no wild cards such as private cars acting erratically, the Bow River environment of trees, bushes, small animals, and pathways to the riverbank is allowed to inch up into the town. Access to this riverine environment would have been impossible with the freeway plan. For Atkins, the river is a true parkway, a fairly radical concept for the time, given that the city wanted the Bow River banks to be major roadways, something it more or less achieved with Memorial Drive on the north bank.

In the spirit of 1950s urban renewal, the City of Calgary

---

1   See J.B. Hedges, *The Federal Railway Land Subsidy Policy of Canada* (Cambridge: Harvard University Press, 1934) for the outline of the Waterways Treaty.

had appropriated and demolished most of the housing in the east end — an economically challenged area, as it mainly housed CNR workers for the East Calgary terminal. The City Hall, a hunched 1907 sandstone gothic building, anchored the southern corner of a new zone of institutional buildings: the library, the police station, the remand centre and court house, the Board of Education building, and the Catholic Separate Schools building across the street, all built in a three-to-four-storey *béton brut* style, grey and louring. Of this development, Atkins said, as only a young architect can,

> The civic centre of library, police station, city hall, parking and administration building as a symbol of functional expression is a failure. Abandon all this for office space and get a new people centre at Buffalo Stadium site on the 4th street axis.

The Buffalo Stadium had been built by the Calgary Brewery in the 1930s on the south bank of the Bow River in what is now known as Eau Claire. Buffalo Stadium was made up of picnic grounds, baseball diamonds, and winter skating rinks. Despite the loss of the East Calgary residential fabric and thus the people who had used Buffalo Stadium, its site was, Atkins believed, a powerful community space already embedded with a kind of civic corpus that would have drawn power away from the old CPR landscape while remaining outside the new-but-deadly bureaucratic landscape of urban renewal around City Hall.

Through all of Atkins's critique is a powerful affection for Calgary that allowed him to rethink the implications of the pressure to develop Calgary as a standard American city — pressure that came with the influx of the Midwestern American oil industry.

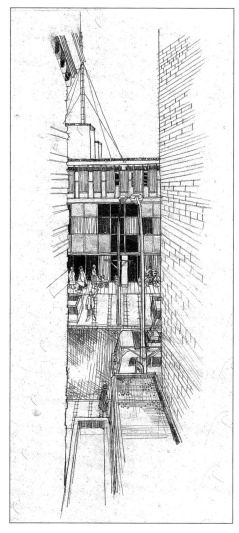

Figure 4-1. There are a number of key indications here of a 1960s Calgary urbanism. The corniced building on the left is sandstone; on the right, brick. Across the street is a low infill building very much like the Beatson Finlayson project described in chapter 39. Atkins has widened the sidewalk, narrowing the roadway to a couple of lanes, one of which is taken up by an electric bus. The downtown has babies in buggies, bicyclists, people hailing taxis, shoppers — it is a generous urban precinct.
Gordon Atkins fonds. Canadian Architectural Archives, University of Calgary. 263A/99.02, ATK A63-01.

[28] Unbuilt Calgary

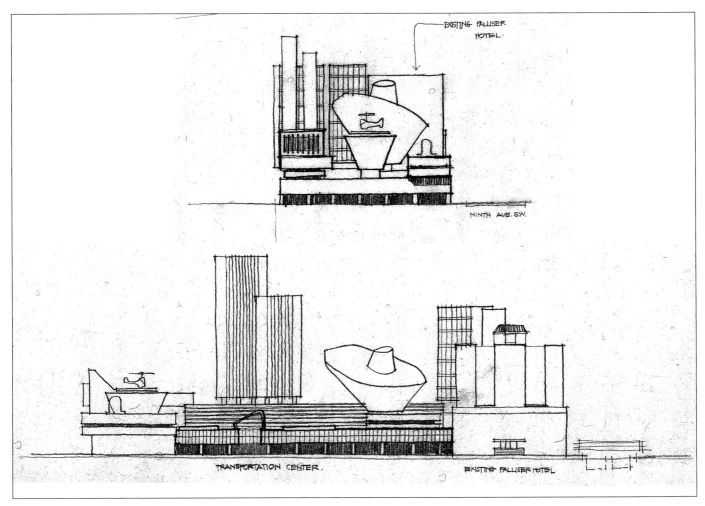

Figure 4-2. Atkins was not happy with the sculptural nature of the New York consultants' proposals for the CPR station site. We don't have this original proposal, only Atkins's response to it, which was to view such an architecture as completely alien, and in this, compared to Bill Milne's attitude to new forms, he is deeply conservative. One could say that Gordon Atkins wanted a Calgary modernism, a Calgary urbanism, note borrowed from somewhere else with a different historical trajectory.

Gordon Atkins fonds. Canadian Architectural Archives, University of Calgary. 263A/99.02, ATK A63-01.

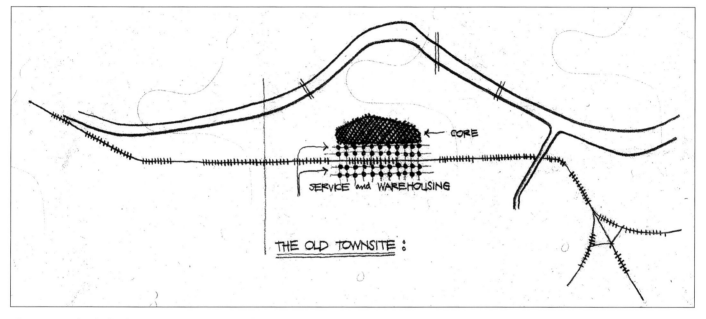

Figure 4-3. This little diagram reoccurs throughout Atkins's analysis drawings. There is a historical logic here that kept the core intense and compact. Although by the 1960s it had expanded to the east, west, and north, the core was still held back from expansion to the south by the CPR main line. Removal of the tracks to the Bow River, as seen in chapter 13, to which Atkins is responding here, would diffuse the downtown core, removing its urbanity.

Gordon Atkins fonds. Canadian Architectural Archives, University of Calgary. 263A/99.02, ATK A63-01.

Chapter 5

The Promotion of Calgary

W.G. Milne, originally from Winnipeg, moved to Calgary after qualifying as an architect following the Second World War. He, too, is an important postwar figure in Calgary: if someone said it couldn't be done, that spurred Milne to prove that it could. He was a relentless, prolific, and effective proselytizer for a modernist Calgary. Milne and Atkins were not the only architects in Calgary, but they were the ones that appear to have generated critiques, oppositional plans, and speculative work.

Milne's files, in the Provincial Archives of Alberta, are extensive; seemingly every letter he ever sent to the City of Calgary, to the newspapers, and to the Chamber of Commerce to suggest and promote new ideas, was saved. He suggested a tower for Calgary, one of the many projects in the run up to Canada's Centennial year in 1967. In October 1963, Milne wrote to the editor of *The Albertan*, responding to an editorial about Calgary's centennial project:

It most certainly should be something which can be admired and shown with pride; a bit of a frill, something we should not otherwise have, of some functional value and of permanent significance. It should also be visually apparent; an integral part of our day to day life and available to all. The Paris Eiffel Tower, New York's Statue of Liberty, Stuttgart's Tower and Seattle's Space Needle all satisfy these requirements and, by their very height, have become architectural pivots and major features of their skylines. A Centennial Tower for Calgary could become the most important element in the city and give our growing core a dramatic accent of monumental proportions. It would be an exciting, imaginative memorial from which every citizen could see the city in its entirety and treat his visitors to a meal in a spectacular manner.

This tower could be a bold stroke which would truly catch the Calgary spirit.[1]

This last line could have been written yesterday, as the city is now engaged in a debate as to whether the white Smithbilt hat is still an appropriate symbol of the Calgary spirit. The 2011 rebranding of the city uses the phrase "Calgary, catch the energy." The city wants to reify this intangible thing, the Calgary spirit, in hats and hockey arenas, lashed to the old West, while participating at the highest level in the geopolitics of energy production.

The 1960s was a critical decade in Calgary, one in which it changed from being a CPR town based on ranching, wheat farming, brewing, and rail yards connected to Canada and Britain in an east–west manner, to being an oil town connected to Houston by pipelines and air travel. The roots of Calgary were sliced off as a new, aggressive enthusiasm for American modernism took hold, shoving aside the buildings and manners of old Calgary. It was a great time to be an architect, as Bill Milne's exuberant career shows.

The tower was built, but not by Milne and not on any of the sites he proposed. His described "600 foot golden spire" could have gone on any of the "City owned parking lots as it stands on legs at the base, which would take little from the parking area" or on the James Short School site — a sandstone school made redundant by the urban renewal scrubbing going on in downtown Calgary — or at Mewata, the armoury built for the Canadian Militia during the First World War at the west end of downtown, or Buffalo Stadium, made redundant with the loss of housing in the downtown area. Today, these sites seem completely inexplicable, so devoid are they of any sort of cultural, historic, or geographical resonance. They were just available pieces of land — any would do.

Milne proposed that the tower be "welded steel plate, internally braced to withstand wind loads of up to 100 mph," thus sitting lightly on the ground in the manner of the Eiffel Tower. The choice of building material reflects the circumstances of the time, as in the early 1960s, the Canadian steel industry was in its greatest period of expansion, seeing a 73 percent increase in production between 1960 and 1965. This was related to production in the U.S., which was similarly high during the period, due to the need for weaponry, aircraft, and vehicles for the Vietnam War; the girders and rebar for the Interstate Highway System; and the continuing consumer demand for automobiles and appliances. However, the U.S. steel industry faced continual labour unrest, and a 116-day strike in 1959 necessitated new channels for foreign steel imports, a need that Canada was ready to fulfill. Canada's steel industry was self-sufficient and competitive; the Canadian government, guided by C.D. Howe, had pushed it to modernize at a faster rate than the private and more conservative U.S. steel industry and to continually expand, even during the economic slump that followed the end of the Korean War. The Trans-Canada Pipeline project, for example, was designed to stimulate steel consumption, and in 1951 General Motors contracted Algoma to supply steel until 1967 in exchange for long-term financing of the Algoma plant. All of this meant that the Canadian steel industry was well-positioned to be the backup for American steel consumption in the event of protracted

---

1   W.G. Milne fonds, Provincial Archives of Alberta, acc. no. 2008.0411.

[32] Unbuilt Calgary

Figure 5-1. The Calgary Tower somewhere around Knox United. This seems a completely random choice of site, but there was probably an empty lot there. In this aerial view that Milne used to test out various tower locations, the CPR station still exists in its original form and not in the mega project that VIA rail, Palliser Square, and the Husky Tower became. The original document in the Provincial Archives of Alberta looks just like this: a pencilled in tower on a 1960s photocopy. We can compare this to the verisimilitude of Photoshopped renderings of today, and the hugely expensive watercolour renderings of twenty-five years ago, which, for a proposal, might have cost $5,000 or more. This scrubby little drawing says much about the confidence of the idea. It wasn't a vision that needed to be bolstered with convincing graphics.

Provincial Archives of Alberta, Accession Number 2008.0411, Box OCSBx1, 87.

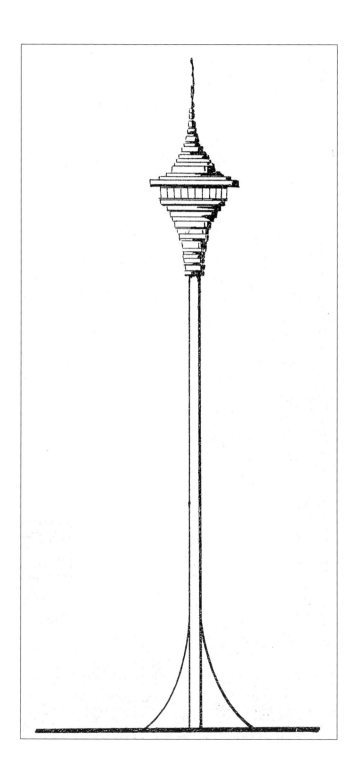

labour unrest. Thus, for a narrow window in the early 1960s, following the end of the 1959 American strike, Canada had a lot of steel available for home consumption.

The Trans-Canada Highway was in construction at this time, and one can still see the overpasses from this era constructed from flat plate steel because it was cheap, and never as cheap again, as even cheaper Korean steel soon became the backup for any steel shortages. This is why Milne's Centennial Tower was proposed as welded steel plate. But Milne did not, in the end, design the tower that was built, although he was instrumental in almost all negotiations leading up to it.

Based on data from Seattle's Space Needle, a vertical steel cantilever structure built for the 1962 World's Fair, Milne estimated that the Centennial Tower would cost $3.5 million and, after operating expenses were deducted from revenue, would maintain an annual $280,000 surplus. Its construction would be financed by a combination of City of Calgary funding, public subscription (similar to the funding for Alberta Gas Trunk Lines), and private investors, despite the admission that the projected return was not high enough for a completely private venture.

Figure 5-2. It is hard to believe today, but this small, relatively crude pencil drawing was the main image of Milne's proposal for a centennial tower. This equivalent of the scribble on a napkin indicates a much simpler time for architecture and ideas. The drawing is, in McLuhan terms, so sparing with its information, that it ignites the imagination just enough to sell the idea, which of course, was Milne's intention.

Provincial Archives of Alberta, Accession Number 2008.0411, Box OCSBx1, 133.

Concurrent to all of this, the CPR was seeking to redevelop its land where the station and the station gardens had been, between 1st Street East and the Palliser Hotel on 1st Street West, a two-block stretch between 9th Avenue and the CPR main line. The CPR's New York architects had already recommended a new commercial/office complex (which so offended Gordon Atkins) to replace the station. Into this stepped Bill Milne with his proposal that the Centennial Tower also be built on the site — and it was, funded by Husky Oil, a Wyoming oil refinery headquartered in Calgary, and Marathon Realty, the Canadian Pacific Railway's land division. Rod Sykes, the assistant general manager of Marathon, wrote to Bill Milne in 1966, complaining that the City of Calgary was interfering with the clarity of the project: "In terms of applying more restrictions to the 9th Avenue traffic and wanting to carve more land off the plaza for traffic purposes — this is not positive thinking. It is entirely negative and it won't get anything built in Calgary."[2]

Rod Sykes was the mayor of Calgary from 1969 to 1977, following Jack Leslie, who had been the aldermanic chairman of the City of Calgary Centennial Committee before becoming mayor in 1965. Leslie was instrumental in keeping the CPR from relocating its tracks to the Bow River. One might say that Leslie was not in thrall to the CPR, and under his watch, as the Sykes 1966 letter to Milne shows, he allowed the City of Calgary to fiddle about with the CPR's redevelopment project.

Like all cities, there are fierce political battles and competing visions when it comes to development; power to effect change or to call for moratoria on development swings back and forth. The tower was built, and it opened as the Husky Tower in 1968 and was renamed the Calgary Tower in 1971. Surprisingly, Milne's cost estimate was accurate: $3.5 million, although the structure was a continuous slipform concrete pour designed by Albert Dale & Associates. Milne was responsible, however, for the spaceship top.

While not strictly an unbuilt project, what is interesting about the Calgary Tower story is its illustration of a postwar civic competitiveness for the highest tower, the tallest building, the biggest tourist draw, and the most heroic vision for aspiring cities. In 1965 Milne made a list of possible names for the tower:

- Sky Spire
- Sky Deck
- Sky Tower
- Sky High Tower
- High Tower
- Arial Tower
- Arial Spire
- Space Deck

None of these names acknowledge the funding realities of such a project. Milne's names are about dreams and aspiration tying Calgary not into industrial or corporate connections but rather to the space race, as happened with the naming of the Atomium in Brussels in 1958 and Seattle's Space Needle of 1960. By the 1970s and the naming of Toronto's CN Tower, such intergalactic romance was gone.

---

2   W.G. Milne fonds, Provincial Archives of Alberta, acc. no. 2008.0411.

Had the tower been built on any of the proposed sites other than Centre Street and 9th Avenue, an impacted site limited by the CPR tracks to its south, it would have acted as a draw to development to the west end of downtown. Subsequent interaction between the CPR landscape and the oil and gas city resulted in a pulling away from the tracks and the old superstructure of the Hudson's Bay, the eastern banks, ranching, and the Grain Exchange, all located on 9th and 8th Avenues and 1st Street. Oil and gas Calgary took off westwards, between 7th and 4th Avenues. The Calgary Tower was left behind in a superseded version of Calgary's economic power base. This gives it, today, a nostalgic quality. It is no longer the tallest thing in the city and is instead more like Calgary's mascot: friendly, familiar, and always in the corner of your eye.

Chapter 6

Seattle World's Fair and the Calgary Tower: The Regional Context

Bill Milne's pitch for a Calgary tower as a tourist magnet was directly linked to the example of Seattle's Space Needle built for the 1962 World's Fair, originally planned as a celebration of the fifty years since the Alaska–Yukon–Pacific Exhibition of 1909. The idea of a festival of the West was left far behind when, in 1957, the U.S.S.R. successfully launched the first satellite, Sputnik, and all of a sudden the U.S. perceived itself as behind in the space race, the battle of innovative science that paralleled the arms race of the Cold War. As a result, Eisenhower announced his intention to prioritize the education of American children in science and technology. Quickly, John Glenn was hurtled into space, just behind Yuri Gagarin. Kennedy then upped the ante, announcing that the newly formed NASA would put a man on the moon by the end of the decade. All of this had a profound effect on the architecture and the momentum of the Seattle World's Fair, officially known as the Seattle Century 21 Exposition.

Seattle's population had increased dramatically during the Second World War as the Boeing Company, founded in 1916 in Seattle as the Pacific Aero Products Company by W.E. Boeing, expanded its aircraft manufacturing capacity; however, it remained primarily a small company town. In 1960 Seattle it had 557,000 people. Calgary, which had also almost doubled its population during the Second World War, had 243,000 people, and did not reach 550,000 until 1980. Vancouver, on the other hand, had 384,000 people in 1960. For Calgary the Vancouver-Seattle axis had always been a powerful tourist destination. Not only was Calgary's population of American citizens leaping ahead with the development of the oil industry, the condition of the as-yet-unfinished Trans-Canada Highway meant that the easiest route to Vancouver was through the United States on its new Interstate Highway System: I-90 going through Spokane, the radio and television hub for American stations broadcasting to southern Alberta, on to Seattle, and then up to Vancouver.

The 1962 Seattle Century 21 Exposition was huge for the United States; it was the apotheosis of American enterprise, innovation, and optimism. President Kennedy opened it by telephone, and astronauts were there. Minoru Yamasaki, who had been born in Seattle, designed Seattle Century 21 Exposition's Science Centre — a system of steel arched webs — and on the strength of this went on to design the World Trade Centre in New York, also structurally based on bundled steel tubes. Was Calgary immune to this enormous event? Certainly not. It was infinitely easier and cheaper to get to Seattle than it was to go to Expo 67 in Montreal just five years later: For Calgary, the psychological and geographical orientation to the West Coast already existed. The Space Needle, as the centre point of the exhibition site, called collectively Seattle Center, was evidently astounding. Milne cites it and the Space Needle's precedents, the Eiffel Tower especially, in his proposal for a similar tower for Calgary. As we know, we did, by 1966, get our tower, with its revolving restaurant, its observation deck, and its UFO imagery. It is the differences, however, that are so telling.

The site chosen for the Husky Tower is impacted. Held in on one side by the CPR main line, on the other by 9th Avenue, to the west by the Palliser Hotel, to the east by MacLeod Trail, there is no room for further expansion. The site has historical significance in its marking of the importance of the Canadian Pacific Railway to Calgary, but it did not anticipate the significant future based on oil and gas extraction; despite the futuristic appearance of the tower, its site is embedded in the early-twentieth-century story of the pre–oil and gas city. The Stampede Grounds, already an exhibition site, was never considered for the Calgary Tower. Nor was Buffalo Stadium considered as a site, probably because of its difficult site conditions: the Seattle Space Needle has thirty feet of concrete ballast beneath it, and the water table of Calgary alone would have made that difficult to achieve. A promising site at the west end of 6th Avenue had available space, as the high-rise city had not extended that far, but it was still a site constrained by the block system of Calgary streets.

Comparing Seattle's tower with Calgary's tower, the political conditions were entirely different. Although Husky Oil financed the Calgary Tower along with the CPR and the City of Calgary, it was a civic project. The Space Needle was embedded in a national project, that of the space race, and although initiated and paid for by local Seattle business interests, the site itself and the exposition had federal funding, thus its development was amplified by its larger political and physical setting.

The legacy of scientific enterprise still exists in the area in terms of technology and innovation: Microsoft, Amazon, Starbucks, Costco, and Nintendo were all developed in the Seattle area. The critical mass of technological championing from the Seattle World's Fair influenced the city almost beyond possibility. For such a small city, Seattle has a disproportionate number of innovative enterprises, based in the legacy of that particular conjunction of local hubris, civic pride, and a national narrative mobilized by the Cold War.

Calgary has local hubris in spades and civic pride to burn, but is not, and never has been, part of any sort of powerful national narrative. This was the reality that led to the 1987 formation of the Reform Party and its slogan, "The West Wants In." Calgary is a de facto part of Canada but was never seen as a city of influence, despite its postwar industrial base, which, the city feels, contributes greatly to the national coffers. The Calgary Tower project was destined to be local. There was not enough external help to parlay it into a scientific, or a cultural, or even an architectural legacy.

The 1964 Calgary Planetarium, another centennial project, was located adjacent to the 1918 Mewata Armoury and Stadium, at the far west end of 6th Avenue. This site, had it also had the Calgary Tower on it, would have perhaps led to a critical mass of exposition buildings. Here, the street grid runs out where the Bow River squeezes close to the CPR main line. It was also one of the early sites considered for the new hockey arena, ultimately built as the Saddledome on the Stampede Grounds for the 1988 Winter Olympics. One might have thought that the Winter Olympics was just the kind of collective event that would have an urban impact at the scale of Seattle Center or Montreal's Expo site, or even the urban renewal process put in place in Vancouver as a result of its Expo 86. The legacy of the Olympics was in winter sports training sites rather than urban form, and its venues were scattered across the city rather than in one critical, generative site.

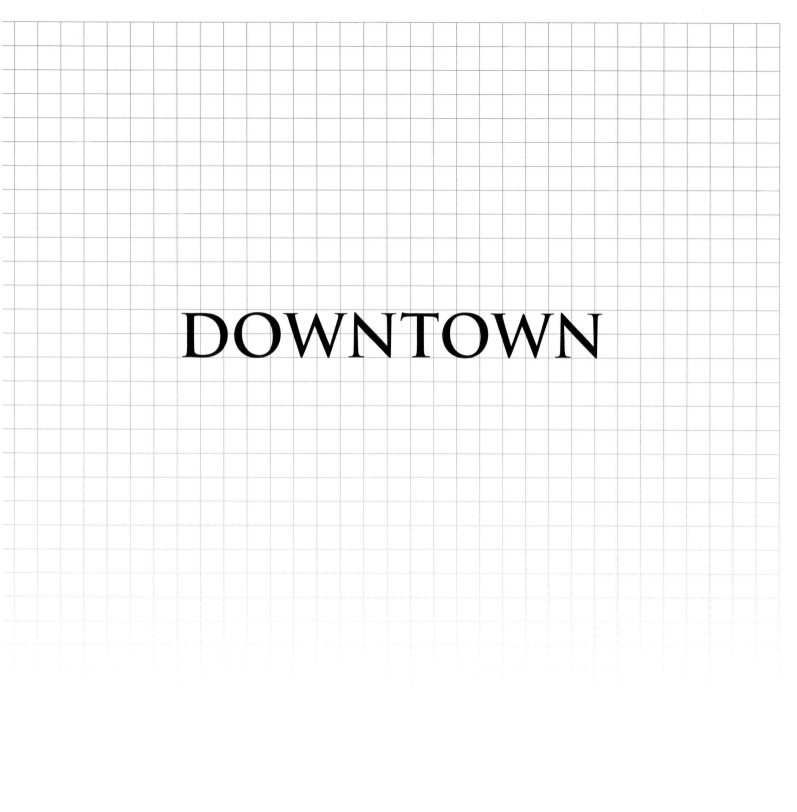

Chapter 7

INTRODUCTION

Calgary is represented by two images: the downtown core — a concentrated island of tall office buildings — and a bucking bronco at the Stampede. One is a physical and spatial reality, the other is a behavioural identity: maverick, fast, and dangerous. The downtown core, which expanded throughout the original city grid, consists of a series of sub-centres, fading in and out of importance with time and changing industrial economies. There is, however, always a larger context for any of the urban changes in Calgary's downtown core. Much as Calgary would like to think of itself as the free-wheeling cowboy on a twisting horse; its plans, built and unbuilt, connect it with deeper urban histories that continue to affect the city today.

To understand Calgary's core, one must first understand the block system, laid out by the CPR, that most of the following plans work with. The CPR was given five hundred million acres in a one-hundred-mile ribbon on either side of the tracks as payment for building the trans-Canada railway, which connected B.C. with Canada and tied down the Northwest Territories and Manitoba. Owning most of the land upon which Calgary was built, the CPR sold parcels in a dense pattern of 25-foot-wide lots, as shown in its 1884 map.

On the floodplain of the Bow River, Calgary's downtown area is flat. The geological conditions that make certain lands ideal meeting places, trails, or paths tend to be the same: flat and fertile with a source of fresh water. Such places are also easy to build upon and underpin most cities. The downtown grid layout did not have to bend around rock outcroppings, although as Calgary expanded, it was laid rigidly upon the map, up escarpment grade changes and over rivers — an abstract ordering system that held until the cul-de-sacs and crescents of postwar suburbia.

Centre Street divides east from west: the east is flat, the beginning of the prairies formed by the Bassano Lake with the melting of the Laurentide ice sheet during the last ice age; the west is the start of the foothills, the once choppy shore of the lake, leading to the mountains. Downtown Calgary sits in a valley formed by the Elbow and the Bow Rivers; at the end of many streets and avenues, one can glimpse the bleached grass of an escarpment, often unbuildable because they are both unstable and steep.

The Canadian Pacific Railway station was on Centre Street, and the avenues were numbered from the point where the Bow River meets Centre Street, locating the CPR tracks between 9th and 10th Avenues south. South of the tracks was a two-block zone of warehouses, workshops, and factories attached to the main line by railway spurs, many of which were still operational in the 1980s. Beyond that were residential neighbourhoods, some that predated Calgary, such as Mission, the site of the Notre Dame de la Paix Oblate Mission, which was founded in 1875. North of the tracks was the designated downtown commercial zone, originally two blocks deep, from 9th to 7th Avenues. Beyond that was a residential district to the river, including Chinatown. At the east the CPR crossed the Elbow River with a bridge, and at the west end of downtown, it made a sharp turn north and proceeded along the Bow River under a steep wooded escarpment now known as Edworthy Park.

Roughly speaking, industrial rail-dependent activities — flour mills, breweries, and hotels — were serviced by 9th Avenue, while 8th Avenue was the shopping street with the Hudson's Bay store, banks, theatres, opera houses, cafés, and restaurants. Churches and City Hall were on 7th Avenue.

Mewata Armouries was built during the First World War at the west end of 8th Avenue, and still exists. At the east end was Fort Calgary, which stood in one form or another from 1875 to 1914, when the land was bought by the Grand Trunk Pacific Railway and turned into a rail terminal. It was reclaimed by the city in 1974, designated a historic site, and the fort was reconstructed. These are the bookends to 8th Avenue.

This little island with its landmarks and tidy history must be kept in mind when we look at all the non-CPR-inflected downtown plans that started to flourish, especially after the 1950s.

Chapter 8

The Thomas Mawson Plan for Calgary

The conjunction of gardens, horticulture, and town planning defines the philosophy of the City Beautiful, whereby social ills can be solved by introducing parks and gardens throughout the city. This kind of architectural determinism has its roots in Jeremy Bentham's philosophy of social reform and utilitarianism, where "the greatest happiness of the greatest number is the measure of right and wrong." Legislation's only use to society is the maintenance of pleasure rather than pain, and to that end, when the industrial city began to be problematized as a behavioural sink that results from overcrowding, the shape of the city became an important condition of this greater happiness — reform of the city and its institutions will lead to the reform of the people in those institutions.

Although Bentham is mostly known now, via Foucault, for his Panopticon prison of 1791 — a drum of stacked cells, a prison of maximum surveillance — such utility can be seen a century later in something so seemingly innocuous and dreamy as Mawson's Calgary plan. And today, although behavioural determinism is felt to be discredited as a social hypothesis, it still exists in urban renewal theory, believing that problematic areas of the city can be reinvented, problematic people relocated, and undervalued land reinvested in. This is precisely the thinking that underpins the Mawson Plan.

When Mawson, an English landscape architect, met Calgary in 1911, probably at the invitation of the Calgary Horticultural Society, formed in 1906, the city had a population of 44,000 — an increase of 960 percent over the 4,000 inhabitants of 1901. Growth was stupendous, unthinking, and expeditious. The Bow River flooded regularly in places; in others it had sawmills, railway yards, and shacks. The downtown centred on the CPR station, the Palliser Hotel, and the sandstone banks and buildings of 8th Avenue, eight safe blocks away from the Bow River.

[44] Unbuilt Calgary

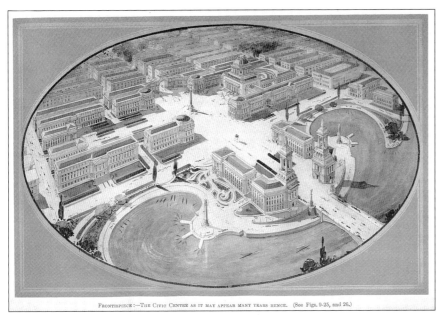

FRONTISPIECE:—THE CIVIC CENTRE AS IT MAY APPEAR MANY YEARS HENCE. (See Figs. 9-25, and 26.)

Figure 8-1. This is the most telling redirection of Calgary away from the landscape of the CPR on 9th Avenue. This, for Mawson, was to be the Civic Centre, a series of plazas and monuments on Centre Street leading to a low, wide bridge over the Bow River. There is a discussion about incursions into the Bow River in chapter 25 with the River's Edge project, where eddies and quiet channels can be cut to increase riverbank frontage and to tame the flow of water into an amenity. However, Mawson's inclusion of rowing eights indicates that he saw the Bow as something like the Thames, rather than the blue-green glacier-fed river it is.
Thomas Mawson. The City of Calgary Past, Present, and Future: A Preliminary Scheme for Controlling the Economic Growth of the City. *London: Thomas H. Mawson & Sons, 1912.*

Fig. 34. · THE C.P.R. STATION PLAZA ·

Figure 8-2. In direct contrast to the reality of the CPR station forecourt shown in chapter three, the company space has been transformed into a civic space: lawn, trees, and a clock tower. No longer is the station faced by scrappy hotels and wooden buildings. Rather, there is an imposing six-storey symmetrical set of buildings flanking Centre Street on the north side of 9th Avenue. The CPR owned this property, and the Marathon Realty Tower was built there in the 1970s, illustrating again the difference between a corporate urbanism and a civic urbanism: different values, different spatiality.
Thomas Mawson. The City of Calgary Past, Present, and Future: A Preliminary Scheme for Controlling the Economic Growth of the City. *London: Thomas H. Mawson & Sons, 1912.*

Mawson proposed an image of Calgary on the Bow derived almost directly from Chicago's Columbian Exposition of 1893. This world's fair was designed by Daniel Burnham and Frederick Law Olmsted as a Beaux-Arts vision of the new American city: white, symmetrical, splendid, and neo-classical. It was an argument for comprehensive city planning over piecemeal, haphazard development driven by land speculation, as was the modus operandi in Calgary. The discourse of the City Beautiful was one of sight-lines and axes, uniform buildings, monuments and flanking public spaces; there was no room for the kind of rhizomatic, anarchic growth based on the self-interest found in a boom town on the Canadian prairies. It seems to have been floated as a material vision to which Calgary could aspire, as it is difficult to conceive of the social and political structures that would have been needed to facilitate Mawson's plan. To enact such a plan would take a Napoleonic force, as happened in Paris in the 1850s under Haussmann, when the old city was buried under ceremonial boulevards, plazas, monuments, and avenues suitable to an imperial capital.

The Mawson plan came at the end of Calgary's building boom, which was succeeded by the First World War, the difficult 1920s, the Great Depression, and the Second World War. By time the next building boom occurred, coinciding with the oil boom associated with the discovery of the Leduc oil fields in 1947, demolished European cities and imperialist ideas were no longer considered models — the U.S. was. And it was a postwar American model, not the 1791 Beaux-Arts plan of Washington D.C., but rather the postwar American city of freeways and suburban development, the space age and libertarianism, that changed Calgary radically.

Chapter 9

Traffic and Parking

Bill Milne was very active in the first oil boom of the 1950s and 1960s, relentlessly and effectively championing a modernist Calgary. He wrote, in a preface to a study of Calgary's increasingly congested downtown core:

> Along with a good number of Calgarians, I have become increasingly concerned with what is happening to the downtown business district.
>
> The traffic, transit and pedestrian problems, and the new outlying shopping centre, all represent threats to the survival of the city centre. The Architect is in a little different position than most people in this respect. Firstly, he has access to information describing what is being done throughout the world regarding these problems, and secondly he has the planning and design background to suggest solutions that suit local conditions.[1]

These two paragraphs could have come from any year since 1960, when it was written. This is the ongoing dilemma for downtown Calgary: there are bigger draws in the suburbs — schools, shopping centres, malls, parks — than the downtown core itself. Yet, all traffic corridors funnel into the downtown, the LRT lines fan out from the core, and the centre is visible from the far edges of the city, a little wedding cake of tiers and towers, dense and intense, clearly the physical heart of the city. Although parking is expensive, it does not act as enough

---

1 W.G. Milne fonds, Provincial Archives of Alberta, acc. no. 2008.0411.

of a disincentive to driving to work, despite the light rail transit and the bus system. Rush hour starts at 6:00 a.m. and again at 3:30 p.m., traffic jams its way in, and nine hours later rams its way out.

Milne complained that there was a traffic light at every intersection in the downtown core, that no one could get anywhere fast and people had to battle cars at every turn. His thesis was that pedestrians and vehicles should mix with one another as in modern shopping centres, with the tempo geared to pedestrians. The entire downtown should be like a shopping centre while curb parking was doubled to 18,000 spaces, resulting in faster traffic. This is all so contradictory that it appears completely mad; however, it deserves unpacking.

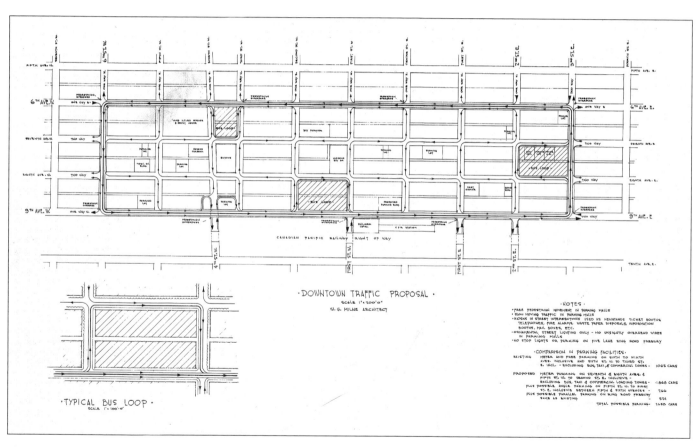

Figure 9-3. How it works: "Free pedestrian movement in parking malls, slow moving traffic in parking malls. Kiosks in street intersections used as news stands ticket booths, telephones, fire alarms, waste paper disposals, information booths, mail boxes, etc. Ornamental street lighting only — no unsightly overhead wires in parking malls. No stop lights or parking on five lane ring road freeway." Total possible parking: 2,650 cars.
Provincial Archives of Alberta, Accession Number 2008.0411.

This plan is based on two main propositions:

1. The Belt Highway, a counter-clockwise ring road that acted as a giant traffic circle without traffic lights stopping and starting the flow of cars. This would leave the downtown free of east–west crosstown traffic.
2. Cross Streets, made very discouraging by forcing drivers to take a zig-zag route from north to south with none of the streets as through-routes. This would have been so enraging that most drivers would have avoided the downtown completely. These cross streets then could have been used for parking.

The economics of this plan have a certain beauty: an alternative eight-hundred-space parking structure would cost the city $1.2 million and the parking would not be distributed evenly throughout the core. Rather, in Milne's proposal, angle parking and a re-designation of existing roads would provide the extra eight hundred spaces needed, and at ground level. The new parking meters would pay for the new curb cuts, which would press the cars into the sidewalk, widening the driving lanes.

The biggest problem would be getting pedestrians across the current of the Belt Highway into what Milne predicted would be a "pedestrian kingdom." The solution is pedestrian overpasses, which, he believed, "would have a spirit of adventure to them," adding that "citizens walking over the bridge could watch the traffic passing underneath." Less expensive would be synchronized walk/don't walk lights on the Belt Highway. These would probably have had more adventure in them than the overpasses.

Streetcars — or their soon-to-be replacement, electric busses — would circle the core on the Belt Highway, pulling off into any of three bus loops for loading and transfers. There would be a maximum of a two-block walk from anywhere in the downtown core to one of these loops.

The absence of honking, idling, polluting, stop-start traffic would allow the cross streets to be largely pedestrian, full of kiosks and year-round vending stands. In this, Milne refers to the mayor's idea of a pedestrian mall, which did come to pass with the pedestrianization of 8th Avenue in 1967. It does indeed have kiosks and vendors, benches and pedestrians, safely isolated from traffic. The difference is that Milne's plan would have spread that easy-going walking street scene throughout the whole downtown core.

Milne's two sketches that accompany this proposal are a delight: he clearly didn't like traffic, but loved cars.

TRAFFIC AND PARKING   [49]

Figure 9-1. This drawing is looking west down 7th Avenue. The Hudson's Bay Company is on the left, its skywalk to the parkade is over the street, and close on the left is Central United Church. Milne has introduced a fine grain of diagonals throughout the city, including angled parking and cross-intersection pedestrian paving with kiosks and planting. It turns a fairly indifferent grid into a series of intimate block-long islands.

Provincial Archives of Alberta, Accession Number 2008.0411.

Figure 9-2. A Beltway overpass separating traffic from pedestrians. Milne thought these overpasses would be quite exciting. His drawing is a bit odd, scale-wise, with only nine or ten steps up and a sloped ramp over the road, where tiny buses and cars have been drawn. In reality, any overpass would be more like the scale of the ones found at LRT stations, with two storeys up, massive construction, and safety standards. This is a lovely image, however, illustrating the thought that traffic could be an entertainment and pedestrian bridges could be so minimal.

Provincial Archives of Alberta, Accession Number 2008.0411.

Chapter 10

The Calgary Civic Centre

In terms of major revision of downtown ordering, we can start with the 1978 plan by Harold Hanen and Raymond Moriyama for the Calgary Civic Centre, the future of which was decided by a public referendum. This was a major architectural project for a new municipal building and a reworking of several blocks around it. Documentation for this project as it was presented to the Calgary public was unusual, consisting of a booklet that lays out the environmental, climate-related, social, and historic conditions for building a new civic centre. These design conditions were theoretical, illustrated by diagrams, and essentially sound. Hanen's interest in winter cities began with this project, leading to his involvement with the Winter Cities Association.

The proposal was backed by a hard plan and a huge massing model of the project. Various civic groups and organizations protested it loudly, mainly on an estimation of its cost, and the debate carried out largely in the *Calgary Herald*. In 1980 the City of Calgary arranged a plebiscite on the project, and it was narrowly rejected.

The Civic Centre proposed a number of block-long low-rise megastructures that included a performing arts centre, the existing Calgary Public Building (the original Government of Canada building on 8th Avenue), and the Burns Building, a white terracotta office building built in 1913, which, while beautiful, was also rundown and full of small offices and artists' studios. The original city hall building was also meant to stay. It did come to pass that the Calgary Centre for Performing Arts occupied the entire block between 8th and 9th Avenues and 1st and 2nd Streets East, incorporating both the Public and the Burns Buildings. This was in the future, however.

Harold Hanen is a difficult architectural figure in Calgary's development. Calgary-born, he ended his career as a great conservationist and was instrumental in the protection and restoration of several historic downtown buildings and Stephen Avenue. This avenue was the original commercial section of 8th Avenue lined with two- and three-storey sandstone and brick buildings built largely between 1900 and the First World War. While Hanen was an employee of the City of Calgary in the 1960s, he introduced the +15 system that now connects most of the downtown with a series of semi-public enclosed bridges at the second storey. The +15 system has been debated ever since. On one hand, it winterizes the city in accordance with Winter City precepts, introducing a weather-protected semi-public retail environment that breaks down the isolation of individual tower blocks. On the other, it guts the importance and the liveliness of the traditional street and public open retail space — the sidewalks and storefronts of the city.

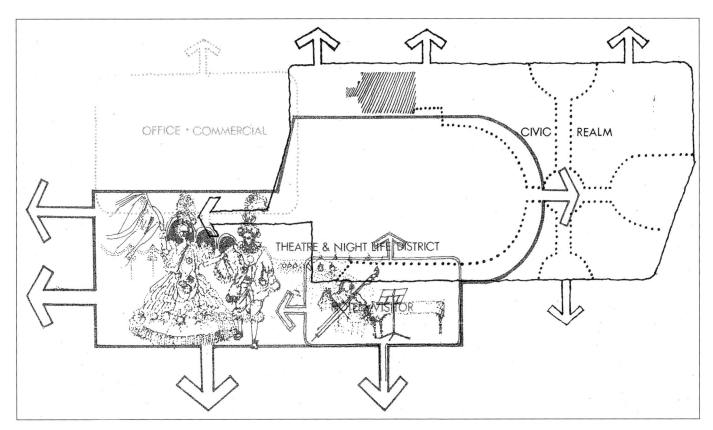

Figure 10-1. In broad strokes, the proposed civic realm wrapped around a large open plaza, which corresponds today to Olympic Plaza. On the south side of the plaza was a theatre and night-life district with a major hotel. This was the zone that became the Calgary Centre for Performing Arts. Office and commercial building are lightly dotted into the northwest corner. The tiny cross-hatched shape centre top is the old City Hall; clearly, the new civic realm was meant to extend well into east Calgary.
Harold Hanen fonds, Glenbow Museum and Archives, M8906-261.

Figure 10-2. Street level views of the massing model, showing the Burns Building (top) in its new context, and below, the central atrium (also see figure 10-4).
Canadian Architectural Archives, University of Calgary.

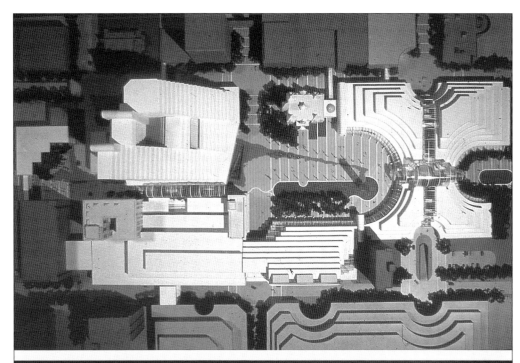

Figure 10-3. The massing strategies for the 1978 Civic Centre are very sculptural. A five-story block, for example, is stepped and carved into a complex ziggurat kind of building. Step-backs allow more light and sun at street level, and they provide roof terraces and break up the scale of what is proposed as very large buildings. This view, by the placement of the old City Hall and the Burns building, shows how much this scheme offered to east downtown. It would have been a critical joint between east and west.
Canadian Architectural Archives, University of Calgary.

Figure 10-4. This could only be the 1970s. This multi-storey atrium bears a close resemblance to Toronto's Eaton Centre, which had just opened, in 1977. This particular space was meant to be threaded into the then-new +15 and +30 walkway system meant eventually to connect all downtown buildings through multiple levels — a three-dimensional street grid.
Harold Hanen fonds, Glenbow Museum and Archives, M8906-261.

Hanen's proposed Civic Centre was straight out of the urban renewal textbook of erasure of historic patterns in favour of civic spatial reorganization into new quasi-ceremonial "gathering spaces." The Civic Centre took four blocks, excavated the central portion for an enormous plaza, and arranged the buildings into a west-facing U-shape. A smaller plaza faced east, continuing 8th Avenue more or less unchanged. Although this plan was rejected, not for its spatiality but for its supposed cost, two parts of it were built: the Calgary Centre for Performing Arts and the Calgary Municipal Building, which dead-ended 8th Avenue before its time.

Both of these plans — the +15 system and the Civic Centre — magnified social polarities in the downtown core. The +15, like the underground malls of most Canadian cities, had the effect of abandoning the ground-level streets and sidewalks to everyone not allowed to use the +15: panhandlers, homeless people, buskers, kids, anyone with dogs, and the poor without reason to trip along the corporate atmosphere all run into private security personnel. In cities without such an alternative pedestrian system, everyone must rub along on busy sidewalks, a clear Jane Jacobs–type definition of a vibrant urbanism. The argument put forth in support of +15 systems is that Calgary's weather demands enclosure, a strangely wimpish reasoning given Calgary citizenry's intense fitness regimes that have people cycling the bike trails into downtown all winter and spending their lunch hours jogging or power-walking those same trails, summer and winter alike. There is a more convincing economic argument, though, in that retail space is doubled: a Starbucks on the street, and one fifteen feet above; two floors of retail mall space rather than just street-level shops. The ultimate illustration of the multi-storey potential of the

+15, +30, and weatherized atria is found in this 1978 proposal — a riot of commingling inside, echoing the celebratory plaza outside.

Before the Municipal Building, the Calgary Centre for Performing Arts, and the 1988 Olympic Plaza across the street from City Hall, 8th Avenue east of Centre Street was a small-scale strip of pawn shops, tailors, junk stores, and coffee shops. City Hall was fronted to the south by a formal park of parterres and benches. In the next block east was the St. Louis Hotel and an eclectic mix of little stores, a gas station, a corner store, some light industrial, a fish market, and a delicatessen. None of it was worth preserving for its architectural quality, but it was evidence that east downtown had been a viable, if lower economic level, community, with 8th Avenue East as its little Main Street.

However, by this time, in the late 1970s, Calgary was in the throes of its second oil boom, awash with disposable income and both embarrassed by and impatient with anything and anybody not participating in the boom. All downtown housing was levelled in preparation of massive high-rise development facing the Bow River; east downtown was gone. With the 1982 crash, it was left as one huge six-by-five-block gravel parking lot, a state in which it remained until 2009 and the advent of the East Village development plan. The destruction of the east downtown Calgary infrastructure, such as it was, was made easier because it had been cut off from the rest of downtown by the sheer eight-storey mirrored glass cliff that was the back of the 1985 municipal building. Out of sight, east downtown didn't even have sentimental value and was soon out of mind. It became a prostitute's stroll, the Safeway became a food bank and then was torn down for more parking, and it passed the 1990s as a drug-fuelled, homeless blot on the downtown core. A set of incongruous senior citizens' apartment blocks facing Fort Calgary and a brave loft-condominium tower were marooned in this social wasteland.

This is the kind of upshot of the sweeping urban renewal projects that so blight the cities that had money to redevelop themselves in the 1960s and 1970s: a deadly era for intelligent urbanism. Although the 1978 Civic

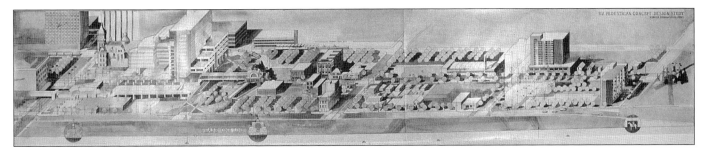

Figure 10-5. This drawing, EV Pedestrian Concept Design Study, shows a +15 8th Avenue extension over the present parking lots and LRT open chasm, depositing people directly onto the block that contains the St. Louis Hotel. The roadway directly behind the Municipal Building becomes parkland; in fact, the whole two-block-wide 8th Avenue section is heavily treed, a quiet oasis behind the civic machine of the Municipal Building.

Harold Hanen fonds, Glenbow Museum and Archives, M8906-261.

Centre is a case of an unbuilt project for Calgary that had long-lasting consequences by simply planting visual and spatial seeds in the public consciousness, not all those seeds germinated, including the important 8th Avenue east–west link. What was acted upon was the strong west-facing orientation of the project in general. Unbuilt never means unimportant or ineffective.

Many years later, in the 1990s, when the problem of east downtown could no longer be ignored, Harold Hanen proposed a continuation of 8th Avenue with a three-to-four storey streetscape similar to Stephen Avenue. It would be a Main Street for a new community, something that coincided with New Urbanism projects being built on the outer edges of Calgary at the time, such as McKenzie Towne. Pressure to develop what is now called the East Village as a medium to high-density community has led to a number of proposals, the most recent of which recommends re-opening 8th Avenue through the Municipal Building, reconnecting east downtown with the downtown core.

Chapter 11

Relocation of VIA Rail Terminal

Despite the rejection by plebiscite of the Hanen/Moriyama Civic Centre plan, its outlines remain. Clearly, it was going to be built, but in a piecemeal fashion rather than as a grand project. It lay as a kind of ghost project, with many future proposals deferring to its unbuilt massing and programming.

One such project is the 1980 proposal to relocate the VIA rail station to Marathon Realty–controlled land east of 3rd Street East. Marathon was the land division of the CPR and for this project used Chandler Kennedy, the architecture firm that developed out of Arthur Dale's practice (Dale was the de facto designer of the Husky Tower, friend of Rod Sykes, the head of Marathon in the 1960s— by this time Sykes was the mayor of Calgary). The proposal placed a VIA Rail terminal in a large tract of CPR land on the south side of 9th Avenue and 3rd Street east that has, since the 1980s, been variously used as a rail car repair yard, as parking, and as an empty gravel bed. At present, the land has been folded into the southern edge of the massive East Village plan.

The drawings for this project show a very large complex that combines VIA Rail with parking, the soon to be built LRT, a relocated Greyhound Bus Station, Calgary Transit, a transport hub to the Calgary International Airport, a car rental outlet, a +15 link, and a shuttle service to downtown. This last is confusing, as downtown, marked in the proposal as radiating around the Petroleum Club at 5th Avenue and 2nd Street West, rather than the old centre of the CPR station or the Hudson's Bay, is only a ten minute stroll away, practically next door in Manhattan terms, but too far, evidently, to walk in Calgary. This indicates an inability, in 1980 to think of downtown Calgary as a pleasant pedestrian city. There are echoes of Gordon Atkins's 1963 proposal for a transportation hub that combined all kinds of systems, although he had placed this in the centre of the downtown core rather than on the then-shabby eastern margin of the downtown core. The 1980 VIA Rail relocation would have revitalized this area beyond recognition.

Had it happened, this, too, would have been the project that jumped the tracks and attached the Stampede Grounds directly to the downtown core, and in this, too, it differs from Gordon Atkins's vision of keeping the core intact as a little island bounded by rivers and the CPR main line. The Chandler Kennedy proposal saw a linkage from Lindsay Park — a downtown sports centre built on the site of the Canadian National Railway terminus — to the Stampede Grounds, to the new VIA Rail station, to Hanen and Moriyama's proposed Civic Centre, to the Glenbow and the 8th Avenue pedestrian precinct flanked by the Hudson's Bay store, the two-block-long Scotia Centre and Toronto-Dominion Centre shopping mall and Eatons at the far west end. The need for linkage is so palpable, so intense in all the civic plans of this era — Calgary needed to be centred, everything linked into a coherent urban network. Diffusion, dispersal, and decentralization were simply not in the discussion.

VIA Rail itself was cut drastically in 1981, under the Trudeau government, with a 40 percent reduction in operations, reducing the two transcontinental passenger trains (one for the northern route, the old CNR tracks, and one for the southern, the CPR tracks) to just one train, with cuts mostly applied in western Canada and the Maritimes. These cuts were reversed briefly in 1984 under Mulroney, but in 1989 Mulroney's budget slashed VIA's funding deeply, resulting in a 55 percent reduction in operations. The transcontinental train route was moved from the CPR southern route, through Calgary, to the northern CN route through Edmonton, severing Calgary from CPR's public face, its passenger rail system. This also contributed to the symbolic isolation of Calgary from central Canada, promoting an even greater feeling of alienation in Alberta than had previously existed. The founding of the Reform Party in Calgary in 1987, while all this was happening, splintered conservative Canada, specifically in protest over the policies of the Mulroney Progressive Conservative government, which the Reform Party felt deferred unreasonably to central Canada, throwing western Canada, a common but misleading euphemism for Alberta, under the train.

One can almost see the late 70s/early 80s plans for Calgary and the desire for a tight centralized city as the construction of a fort, a defensive city form. Calgary's reputation as a law unto itself has always been supported by its financial independence, drawn from its oil and gas reserves. With the severing of the symbolic and

Figure 11-1. Here is another of those tall, fun-filled atrium-gallerias — much larger of course than the one proposed for the Civic Centre — drawn in the bottom view from Southeast. This project straddles the railway tracks, for three blocks. Southeast Calgary was always the industrial quadrant, based on the CPR. This perspective shows the three power bases in the city: the newly relocated CPR, pulling to the southeast and filling a significant territory of east Calgary; the newly proposed Civic Centre occupying six blocks in the direct east of the downtown core; and oil-and-gas Calgary racing away to the northwest of the downtown core. The tower, once the symbol of the CPR and Husky Oil, by this time is a kind of cotter pin in the tripartite core.

Dale Chandler Kennedy fonds. Canadian Architectural Archives, University of Calgary. 1945A/84.15, DAL 82032.

Relocation of VIA Rail Terminal [59]

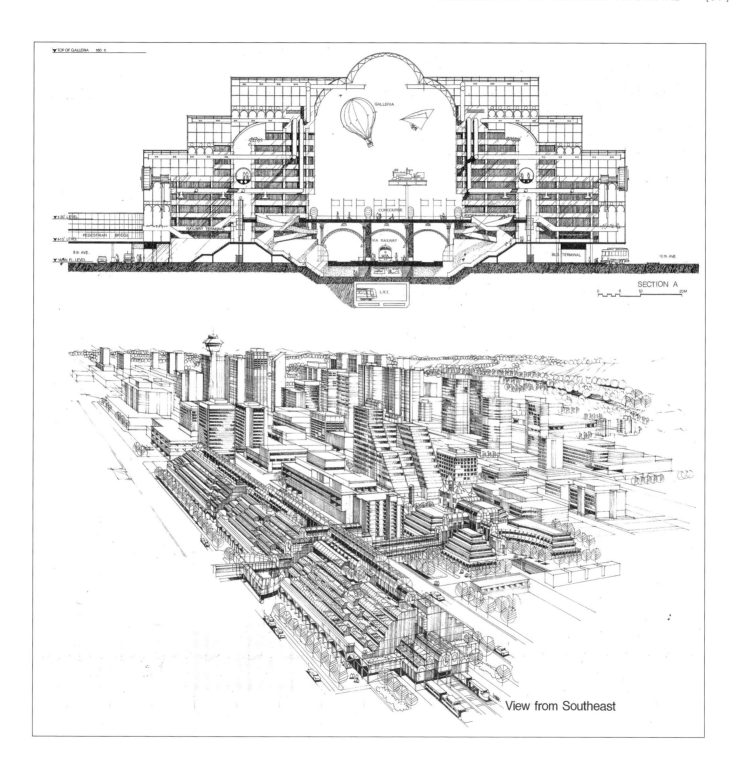

View from Southeast

fairly nostalgic (because hardly anybody other than students and tourists travelled by train at this point) east–west linkage between Calgary and the rest of the country, the city was released to champion its north–south connections. Industrially and corporately, Calgary had more in common with Dallas and Houston than it did with Vancouver or Montreal, from which, at this point in federal-provincial relations, grew the complaint that Alberta was paying more to Ottawa than it received, a sentiment that continues.

What would have been the shape of Calgary had this project been built? It would have changed the orientation of the Municipal Building, chosen by competition in 1981. But then again, maybe not — just by reading plans and observing the placement of significant buildings in Calgary, one can sense a jurisdictional and spatial separation between City Hall and the Canadian Pacific Railway. The post-1960s urban landscape of the oil and gas industry had headed into the west and northwest side of downtown, the CPR and the HBC still held the centre, the City Hall and related civic institutions were located in the east, and even today, through its development of the East Village, the City of Calgary maintains its view of downtown from its eastern bastion. In the end, the CPR as a spatial force was so diminished as to be near invisible. The Palliser Hotel was sold to Fairmont, the passenger trains no longer run, the industries that needed the railway for access and service have long been moved out of the downtown core, and other than the basic street pattern, there is little visible of CPR influence.

Chapter 12

Calgary Municipal Building Competition

The open architectural competition held in 1981 as the first stage for a new Municipal Building drew 143 entries from both Calgary and the rest of the country. It offers a snapshot of architectural thinking during a time of great architectural upheaval in Canada. The Mississauga City Hall competition, held shortly after, was won by Jones and Kirkland, who proposed a city hall separated into a number of programmatic and formal pieces: a silo, a facade, and an arcade, all held together by the consequently intricate public space on the ground plane. The well-publicized Mississauga City Hall competition entries illustrated the currents of postmodern architecture that were in the journals and in the minds of many architects who had entered the Calgary Municipal Building competition. The Calgary entries were not recorded or archived, so in this section we are working from an unlabelled set of slides of the models found in the Canadian Architectural Archives at the University of Calgary. The entries fall into four camps: postmodern, late capitalist modern, diagonal formalism, and a traditional civic formalism. The competition was shortlisted to five entries, then eventually won by Christopher Ballyn and the Webb Zerafa Menkes Houdsen Partnership, and the Municipal Building was built, and opened in 1985.

The site itself fills the two blocks south of the 1911 sandstone Romanesque Revival City Hall, which was made a National Historic Site in 1984. The 1978 Hanen Moriyama downtown proposal had massed a great stepped-back amphitheatre, a galleria, and a vast open public plaza on the site, not unlike the building and plaza eventually chosen in the Municipal Building competition. The original site plan in the competition brief indicates an LRT stop beneath the site, clearly meant to serve City Hall and the Municipal Building. The stop was built but never used.

[62] UNBUILT CALGARY

Figure 12-1.
Michael McMordie slide collection, Canadian Architectural Archives, University of Calgary.

The array of proposals for the Calgary Municipal Building are interesting to look at now, almost thirty-five years later, to think about how the east end of downtown would have been different had any of them been developed and built. From this distance, there are no right or wrong architectural proposals, simply a variety of interpretations of what a city hall for Calgary in 1981 ought to look like. It was a crucial time in the city's history, just before the building boom crashed in 1982.

In the proposals that develop a commercial modernism, the prevailing architectural style at the time in Calgary, the role of the existing City Hall was almost always put forth as a decorative little castle on the northwest corner of the complex, with completely unrelated architectural production filling the rest of the site. The City Hall was treated as something that had to be there because it was in the design brief as some sort of obstructive land form. This sort of thing can work if done deliberately, producing a hybrid condition that slams something very modern up against something very old, but that wasn't quite how it worked in early 1980s Calgary. In the five entries shown here, the program for the Municipal Building, a complex of civic departments and public functions and spaces, was amalgamated into simple, solid blocks. The site is more or less irrelevant, other than as a plinth for a variety of large, solid towers.

For all the competitors, the plaza quickly emerged as the soft centre of the project; the buildings were its backdrop. The floating office building, (b) in figure 12-1, frees the whole site to act as an urban landscape with its own topography, more or less unimpeded by the tower, which is lifted up on piers. This daring Ricardo-Bofill-type solution really diminishes the importance of the old city hall, completely overshadowing it. The City of Calgary was pushing itself forward with this large competition, registering itself in the public mind as a force. It might not have been amused to find its historic City Hall so overwhelmed in this proposal, but the sheer declarative chutzpah of a municipal building in a tower would have had some appeal.

The short eight-storey angular entry in figure 12-1 (c) that wraps around the front plaza treats the City Hall with respect, offering a link through the site to east Calgary in lieu of 8th Avenue continuing through. At the time, though, many people were happy *not* to have a link to it. Now that east Calgary is being redeveloped as the cultural arts heart of the city, the link is missed.

The second major group of entries, figure 12-2 (next page), takes City Hall as the generative motif of the proposal. One project (bi–bii) literally reproduces the mass of the 1911 building in eight pavilions linked by glazed walkways: 8th Avenue becomes a block-long glass house, clearly distinguishable from the rest of the architecture. Another project (ai–aiii) reproduces old City Hall in glass and sits it on the southwest corner of the site so that the two 1911 buildings — the real one and its avatar — are the front faces of a large U-shaped municipal building that wraps around the rest of the site. The plaza leads to a semicircular loggia and a ziggurat false front entry where 8th Avenue would have been. The third entry (c) in this burst of postmodern reference draws from the Nolli Map of Rome, a figure-ground map much in circulation in the early 1980s that privileged open space over buildings. An interesting false perspective is set up by putting a little temple entrance at the very back of the site up a wide ramp, its axis skewed off the north-south grid orientation by a massive building on the south side of the site. Interestingly, this temple idea reappears in the 2005 East Village Area Redevelopment Plan, albeit

[64] Unbuilt Calgary

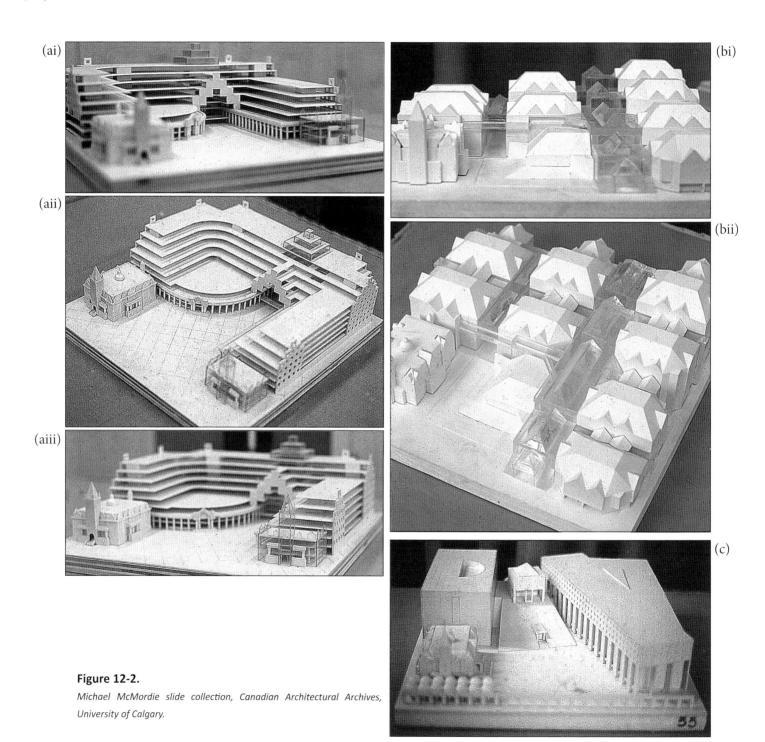

Figure 12-2.
Michael McMordie slide collection, Canadian Architectural Archives, University of Calgary.

facing east. The 1960s extension at the back of the old City Hall is replaced by a sculptural solid, a move much like the one that so annoyed Gordon Atkins twenty years earlier, anchoring the northeast corner. MacLeod Trail is screened by a semi-loggia facade; City Hall rests like a gently faded elderly lady amidst all this robust power and 8th Avenue is deep-sixed.

The next four projects in this small selection of the 143 competition entries, figure 12-3, exhibit a solid, low-rise, formal massing strategy that has none of the whimsy of early 1980s postmodernism, none of the opportunism of the commercial-modern tower projects, and none of the dynamism of diagonal axes — these projects are very serious. What the top three (a–c) have in common is a kind of defensiveness and a privatization of the public plaza: two (a and b) bury it in the middle of the building as a courtyard, while the other (c) screens it from view with a heavily planted urban forest. The second project (b) opens the courtyard to the south and is one of the few entries to make a point about challenging the orientation that was set out so clearly in the Hanen and Moriyama Civic Centre proposal of 1978. At the same time, it gives the old City Hall its own south-facing plaza balanced by a sunken courtyard amphitheatre. The east-west conventions of the site, found so clearly in the bottom entry (d), are reoriented into a north-south display. All of these entries appear massive. Their particular kind of postmodernism borrows much from perimeter-block Berlin, another model much published at the time. Plunging into the projects as a pedestrian route is 8th Avenue, which emerges in various plazas and courtyards and slips into east Calgary at the back.

Of the entries with strong diagonal orientations, figure 12-4, one of them, (b), was chosen as the winner and actually built. In the three projects shown here

(a)
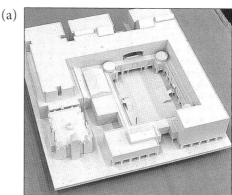

(b)
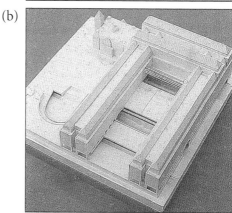

(c)

(d)

Figure 12-3.
Michael McMordie slide collection, Canadian Architectural Archives, University of Calgary.

[66] Unbuilt Calgary

(a)
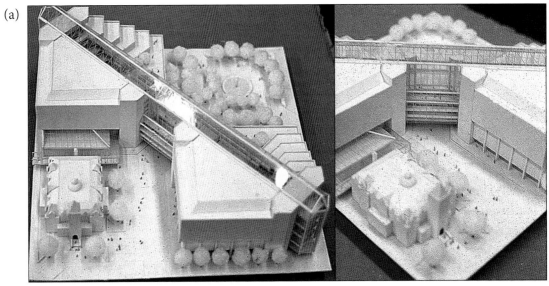

(b)
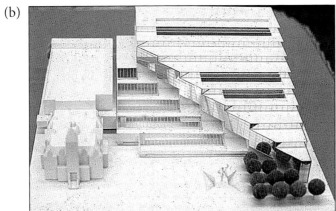

(c)
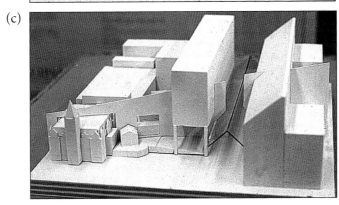

Figure 12-4.
Michael McMordie slide collection, Canadian Architectural Archives, University of Calgary.

(there may have been more, but these are the three that were recorded), a diagonal direction is introduced to the strict north-south/east-west orthogonal grid of downtown Calgary, probably to lend the building a metaphoric dynamism to parallel a dynamic civic political process.

The top project offers the most to the future east Calgary: City Hall on the northwest corner is balanced by a new plaza on the southeast corner — again, there is a reorientation here that is quite elegant in the larger urban conversation in which Calgary is presently engaged. It is interesting to look at which of the 1981 competition entries anticipate Calgary's east side development in the 2000s, and how few of them got it right. As a footnote to the introduction of a sharp diagonal in the Municipal Building, the 2011 East Village Plan by Broadway Malyan added a diagonal axis that kicks off from the corner of the Municipal Building, through the otherwise original orthogonal street pattern of the area. It is the first East Village plan to include this dynamic cut through the grid and makes sense of the Municipal Building diagonal as a directional device.

As this book is about unbuilt Calgary, following the model started by the book *Unbuilt Toronto*, something must be said here about the utter disinterest Calgarians have toward the past. The Calgary Municipal Building competition was important. It was one of a set of three city hall competitions of the early 1980s, including the 1982 Mississauga City Hall competition, and the 1979 Edmonton City Hall competition. The Calgary Municipal Building competition came and went without a trace, save for five entries of the second stage that one can find on the web, and the project that was actually built. The City of Calgary Corporate Records, the archives where one would expect to find the results of the competition, did not record any of the original 143 entries, and the Canadian Architectural Archives did not collect the drawings that accompanied the models. The Calgary Municipal Building competition's absence from the public record is pretty complete. And this is where, perhaps, Calgary diverges from cities such as Toronto, or Halifax, or Victoria. The past is just a means to get to the present. If a project doesn't happen, then throw it away. There are plenty more coming down the pike. In Calgary what could have happened is never considered as interesting as what did happen.

ROADS AND BRIDGES

Chapter 13

South Bow River Parkway

In 1964 the City of Calgary made an agreement with the Canadian Pacific Railway to re-route the CPR main line away from the blocks between 9th and 10th Avenues — the major obstacle to southern expansion of the downtown core. The drawings accompanying this agreement propose a traffic corridor of railway and roadway on the south bank of the Bow River. This is perhaps the last time that the Bow River was understood as a throwaway feature rather than as an amenity. It is difficult to understand now how a river could be treated this way by both city and industry. Ordinary Calgarians of the time didn't think of the Bow River as an entirely industrial channel; its little islands were campsites, and Buffalo Stadium was on the river and deeply loved. However, the new road and rail scheme obliterated any houses on the river, including Chinatown, and it ploughed through Inglewood: it was the apotheosis of the Robert Moses planning ethos that favoured urban freeways over any other kind of transit.

A 1930 aerial photograph shows the Imperial Oil refinery, part of the wedge of industry that lines the Bow River east of downtown Calgary. At the time of the freeway plans and rail corridor relocation, this refinery was still in operation; Alyth Yards, the CPR marshalling yards, grain terminals, light industry, gravel mines, concrete plants, and, since the late 1980s, south Deerfoot Trail, line the river. There was strong a precedent for discounting the Bow River as an amenity, thus it was easy to extend its industrial nature into the heart of downtown Calgary as one massive freeway, rail, and trucking system.

These plans, when released, were a very large cat let loose among the stakeholder pigeons in east Calgary. The issue led to the establishment of the first community association, in Inglewood, and in its original form, an activist community planning body that protested the rape of both their neighbourhood and the Bow River by

[72] Unbuilt Calgary

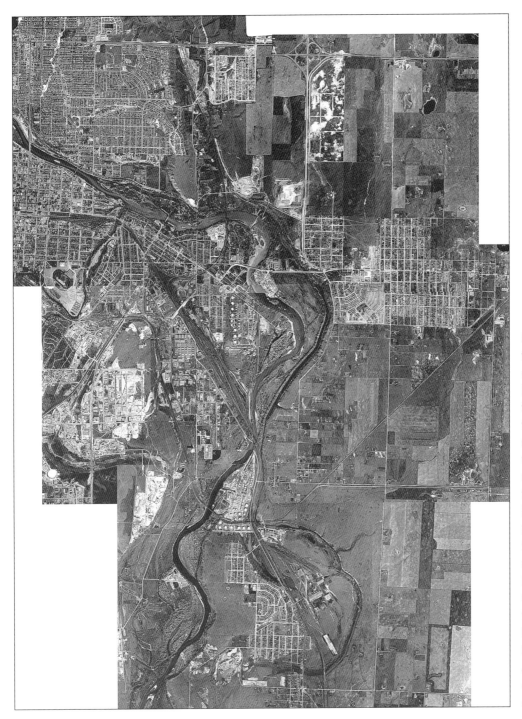

Figure 13-1. In 1959, just before the extensive changes to the city of the 1960s, we can see how impacted the Bow River was in the southeast quadrant. Toward the south is the oil refinery shown in figure 13-2. Each industrial installation has a small community of houses nearby. About two-thirds of the way up on the left-hand side, one can see the Stampede grounds and the racetrack, and part of the CN depot directly west of it. Across the Elbow River, to the southwest of the Stampede, is a large industrial area that abuts Cemetery Hill and Burnsland Cemetery. This is industrial still.

Aero Surveys Photography. Panchromatic aerial photography of the City of Calgary and surrounding area, 1:18,000, 1959.

Figure 13-2. How not to treat a river, especially the Bow River, an ancient First Nations highway on the migration route of many birds, a river that floods and that carries on until it joins with the Oldman River to form the South Saskatchewan. The South Saskatchewan crosses the prairies to Hudson Bay. The Bow River Water Council, established only in 2004, now monitors the river and its watershed.
Courtesy Library and Archives Canada, PA-015634.

the CPR and the City of Calgary. One can date a new awareness of Calgary's potential to be a liveable city from this precise time. No longer would it be acceptable to privilege transportation over neighbourhoods.

In 1961 Jane Jacobs published *The Life and Death of Great American Cities*, in which she outlined the opposition to the prevailing Robert Moses view of building large road systems to deliver thousands of suburban automobiles to the downtown business core. Her example of the liveable city was Greenwich Village, a small neighbourhood in Manhattan that had a diversity of economic levels, ages, services, and building fabric. The fabric of a city can be fine-grained or coarse. The fine-grained texture of a city composed of small neighbourhood units, socially responsible for their futures, underpins almost all the subsequent Calgary community Area Redevelopment Plans. It took a crisis of such crass dimensions as the South Bow River Parkway to jolt Calgary into the realization that the city is a fragile thing, easily destroyed.

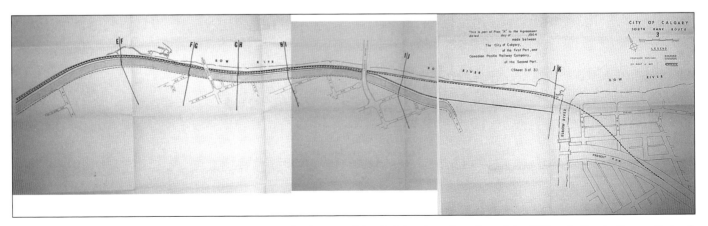

Figure 13-3. Part of the agreement between the City of Calgary and the CPR for the relocation of the CPR main line to the south bank of the Bow River.

Assembled from drawings in Community Heritage, Calgary Public Library.

Chapter 14
Centre Street Bridge

Many unbuilt projects for Calgary were sometimes realized in a different configuration or on an adjacent site, so in one sense they were built, but here are sometimes curious inclusions in the original propositions that indicate certain social attitudes to things such as nature, or rivers, or transportation that are obscured by the ongoing presence of buildings and development. A case of such is the Centre Street Bridge, approved in 1912 and finished in 1916. Famously, this is one part of the Thomas Mawson plan that was actually built. Mawson conceived of Calgary as Vienna on the Bow: Vienna had placed its arts and cultural buildings, as well as its administration and institutional buildings, in a ring around the city — Calgary could do that, it had a ring of escarpments. The City Beautiful, Haussmann's Paris in miniature, could lead, for Mawson, to axes, monuments, crescents and a series of formal interventions in the relentless planning grid first laid down by the Dominion Survey and filled in by CPR engineers.

Mawson produced a report, *The City of Calgary Past, Present, and Future: A Preliminary Scheme for Controlling the Economic Growth of the City*, printed in London in 1914, full of drawings and watercolours of a Calgary-to-be, a polychromed, swirling metropolis to be built out of the burnt grass, river silt, and prairie winters at the confluence of the Bow and the Elbow Rivers. And there the plan rested. Then, miraculously, in 1977, Mawson's large original drawings and watercolours were found mounted on board, lining a garage in Eau Clair on the south bank of the Bow River. Had it not been for the demolition of downtown Calgary residential neighbourhoods in the 1960s and 1970s, the original Mawson drawings would not have been found.

The Mawson plan had been done and paid for near the end of the wheat boom that crashed in the run-up to the First World War. A number of devastating events followed the war, including the Spanish Influenza pandemic of 1918 and all of the problems associated with returning soldiers: unemployment, poverty, homelessness, and the Winnipeg Riot. The 1920s in Canada were both violent and desperate. By the end of that decade came the economic crash that led to a world-wide depression, including the 1935 On to Ottawa Trek and the Regina Riot — a depression unrelieved until the start of the Second World War. Building during the 1930s in Calgary happened downtown with make-work projects for banks, government buildings, and schools. There was no place for the hubris of Mawson's European visions for Calgary, and the drawings were only worth the boards they were pasted on, useful for the lining of a garage.

Nonetheless, the rediscovery of the Mawson drawings in 1977 coincided with the emergence of both postmodern classical architecture and the related New Urbanism, architectural movements embraced enthusiastically by Calgary architects in the early 1980s. Calgary still has some lovely examples of residential postmodernism, and McKenzie Towne, an exurban neo-traditional community begun in 1995, involved Andrés Duany, the designer responsible for the urban code of Seaside Florida (a code that specifies density, building details, lot coverage, land use, and setbacks in a way that prevents wasteful and uniform suburban development). And even later, the 1990–2000s conversion of the Canadian Forces Base Currie Barracks turned a low-density postwar military landscape of small PMQs (Personnel Married Quarters for the Canadian Forces) into a beautiful and successful New Urbanism neighbourhood. This turn away from modernism in Calgary was supported by the discovery of Mawson's plan, which reintroduced a formality to residential development, with proper streets, blocks, and parks of Victorian propriety. It was extremely attractive compared to the reality on the ground in the late 1970s, which involved the pretty rapacious development of minimal townhouses on one hand and early monster houses on the other.

Centre Street Bridge, with its north-facing concrete lions copied from the lions in Trafalgar Square, is on axis with the Calgary Tower, at Centre Street and 9th Avenue. If one approaches the city from the north on Centre Street, the tower marks the core from at least a mile away, and as one tips over the edge of the escarpment to the Bow River, one sees the Centre Street Bridge, flanked by lions, leading into the downtown core. It is dramatic, moving; it makes the heart lurch every time. It almost didn't happen.

The City of Calgary commissioned Thomas Mawson's plan, possibly to counteract the dominance of the Canadian Pacific Railway, which had acted with impunity in terms of its own land at the heart of most of western Canadian cities from Winnipeg to Vancouver. The City of Calgary, however, did not have the deep pockets of the CPR — cost was and is always an issue. Mawson had proposed a low-level bridge rather than the high-level bridge actually built. The bridge that was built, on axis with Centre Street, crosses the Bow River at an angle, so is almost twice as long as it would be crossing the Bow River at the right angle approved by the City of Calgary. This, however, would have put it out of alignment with the street grid, losing the ritual importance of a formal entrance to downtown Calgary. It was the spirit of Mawson's plan, rather than the details, that the City of Calgary recognized, and although it didn't have the wherewithal to implement Mawson's entire vision, the first infrastructure project built after the plan was published was the 1916 Centre Street Bridge.

The re-orientation of a bridge is a very small point, hardly worth investigating if it didn't indicate a desire for Calgary to appear important and careful of its image. Today one would say it has always wanted to punch above its weight, confident that it would grow into that weight and the infrastructure would already be there.

The expeditious right angle crossing would never have captured anyone's imagination.

The alternative crossing drawing that actually went to the City of Calgary for planning permission — a fragile thing found in the City of Calgary archives and too delicate to reproduce — shows some interesting details.

Fig. 18.—The "Low Level" Bridge at Centre Street.

Figure 14-1. The low-level bridge at Centre Street.
Thomas Mawson. The City of Calgary Past, Present, and Future: A Preliminary Scheme for Controlling the Economic Growth of the City. *London: Thomas H. Mawson & Sons, 1912.*

The grade change at 5th Avenue, where the ground fell away to the river channel, probably flooded in spring due to melting snow in the mountains and, in summer, with storm run-off. A small iron bridge already crossed the river, connecting 1st Avenue and Centre Street with a pathway on the north bank under the escarpment that met the river bank at this point: there was very little room between river and cliff. To get from 5th Avenue South to 5th Avenue North, across the Bow River Valley, was a massive engineering project, which, when completed, left the river environment largely untouched. Had the short bridge been built, it would have involved a different kind of engineering, creating a roadway on unstable and flood-prone ground, and it would have filled the river environment with roads and streetcar lines, something that eventually happened with Memorial Drive, but only after the Bow River was stabilized by reinforcing its banks.

The present-day program of Bow River footbridges is more in the line with this original proposal: structures built just above the river's high flood levels and for relatively light loads. In building the longer Centre Street bridge, in concrete, arched and buttressed, the city was building for a future half a century away.

Chapter 15

St. Patrick's Island Bridge

The current urban footbridge phenomenon began in the late 1990s. International in scope, the footbridge, with its light active loads, has become an architectural set piece that brings fame to cities seeking recognition for forward-thinking design. Footbridges are a small, relatively inexpensive opportunities for extravagant architectural expression. London's program of millennial footbridges over the Thames was the first sustained footbridge program of the new century. Many bridges have followed, in an international bridge boom recognizable in the career of the Spanish architect and engineer Santiago Calatrava, who was given a contract by the City of Calgary for a bridge from Eau Claire across the Bow River to the footpath alongside Memorial Drive. It opened in 2012 after many construction delays. Because of controversy over the construction and the ballooning cost, the next bridge, crossing from the Memorial Drive footpath over the west end of St. Patrick's Island and arriving at Fort Calgary, was chosen after a competition and awarded to RFR, a French design engineering firm.

The opportunities in an open competition differ from regular commissions. On the sheer strength of design, a shortlist is chosen. There is a complication however, in that some provincial architects associations do not allow their members to do any pro bono design, and unfortunately competition entries, which require a design commitment in both time and material (a project must be more or less designed simply to demonstrate that it is viable), fall into this pro bono category. Thus, local architects are discouraged from entering these competitions, although some do, nonetheless. The St. Patrick's Bridge competition was a chance to compete with international architects of the stature of Calatrava or RFR — an almost unheard of opportunity. And this raises, in the long term, a city's design sensibility.

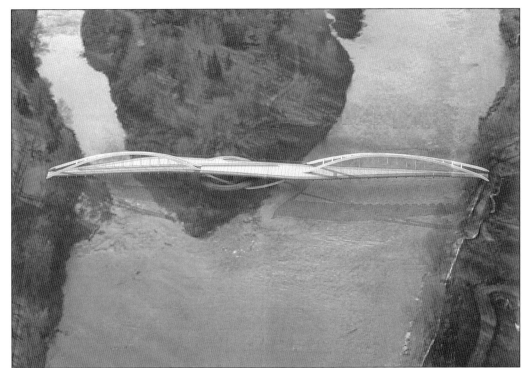

Figure 15-1. The plan of this bridge, the lower drawing, shows that the shape of the bridge deck does not conform to the structural pieces. In most bridges the structure defines the outer edges of the deck: bridges are roads either hung from a superstructure, or supported by piers below. In this bridge there is a centre path, but also wide bays cantilevered off the edge of the structural arches, so that people can step out of the flow of traffic.
Manu Chugh Architects and Planners, Calgary, Alberta.

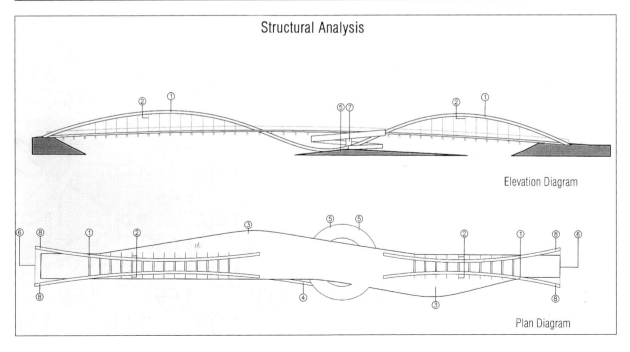

The 2009 St. Patrick's Bridge competition was set by the Calgary Municipal Lands Corporation as part of the East Village project. It was looking for the best architectural solutions, with no particular preference given to the local community, signalling Calgary's status as a city cognizant of international design standards and architectural value: may the best design win. Similar competitions have brought Calgary a number of new projects by international architects who form temporary partnerships with local firms that look after the project on the ground.

Many of the St. Patrick's Island Bridge competition entries were exciting feats of engineering. Piers carried suspension cables in huge swooping arcs, and structural components shot off in orbit around what is essentially a footpath lifted off the ground. The chosen RFR bridge is a thin ribbon that bounces across the Bow, touching lightly on St. Patrick's Island.

One of the entries not chosen is another beautiful ribbon that consists of a double arch that hovers over the western tip of St. Patrick's Island. Manu Chugh Architects and ISL Engineering and Land Services proposed two arches, one from Memorial Drive to St. Patrick's Island, and the other from St. Patrick's to the south bank of the Bow. The bridge deck hangs from these arches, and for the short distance between the two arches, corresponding to the section actually over the island, the deck is supported by a concrete spiral ramp that acts as an abutment for the ends of the arches, and a way to get off the bridge and onto the island. What is especially graceful about this design is that the shape of the deck is not contained by the structural arches and hangers but escapes from the structure to form wide cantilevered planes over the river. One can stop, think, contemplate the water, or fish, or wait in the sun without being jostled by joggers and cyclists shooting across the bridge, a problem with much of the Calgary pathway system of which these bridges form a part.

There was an interesting lighting component to this proposal. Rather than having the bridge ablaze all night, lighting responded to changes in the live load on the bridge deck. Heavy usage, lots of people, lights are bright. At two in the morning, no people, lights are dim. This kind of reflexivity of use presents both sustainability and a kind of provisional responsiveness that is very attractive. We often move through our environments without touching them, but this bridge would have acknowledged our presence, something that would have been quite gratifying.

Chapter 16

Fish Creek LRT Bridge

In 2000 an invited competition was held for an LRT line bridge over Fish Creek, beside an existing early twentieth-century riveted CPR bridge. It seems a perfect site, the old and new transport systems side by side, over Fish Creek as it passes on its way to join the Bow River. Fish Creek Provincial Park is a vast urban park, nineteen kilometres from west to east, where it includes the Bow River. It is completely surrounded by development except for its western edge where it abuts the Tsuu T'ina Nation. MacLeod Trail crosses it, and Deerfoot Trail bottlenecks at its east side.

Just as the confluence of the Elbow River and the Bow was an important meeting site, so too was the point where Fish Creek meets the Bow. There was a trading post and farm there in the 1870s, and then the area was acquired by the Dominion government in 1877 with the signing of Treaty 7 with the Blackfoot as a demonstration farm to teach the nomadic Blackfoot how to be farmers now that they were confined to a reserve. It wasn't successful as a farm and was sold to William Roper Hull, who irrigated the Fish Creek Valley, increasing its hay yield. Renamed the Bow Valley Ranch, it was bought by Pat Burns in 1902. Burns bought all the surrounding farms and ranches until he owned all the land in southeast Calgary, from Fish Creek to the CPR tracks running through the city. The Burns family held Bow Valley Ranch until 1972, when it was sold to the Province of Alberta, and it was made into a provincial park in 1975. At the time, it was quite distant from Calgary, although the city limits had been extended to include it in the 1961 annexation. Fish Creek Park is reputedly three times the size of Vancouver's Stanley Park and is an amenity of great value.

With this history and its special status in Calgary, one would expect a bridge crossing Fish Creek to have some sort of delicacy, something to match the beauty of the land. A bridge is essentially a deck, a continuation of the land, supported in some way so that it continues the ground plane over a canyon, or valley, or any sort of depression. This can be done with a great deal of material, the structural strength determined by sheer weight, or with not much material, the structural strength optimized by its form. The proposal prepared by Tom Martin Consultants consists of two decks that carry the LRT tracks, which are supported by a single concrete-filled steel tubular arch with three sets of V-shaped struts supporting the concrete deck. It is very thin, very elegant; its weight to strength ratio very small. It was never going to be some sort of reconstructed late-nineteenth-century piece of historicism, given that Martin's engineering career started in the London office of Ove Arup in a small team that contained both Arup and Happold, masters of innovative and minimalist engineering design. Martin's idiom is a nimble kind of engineering, seen at its best on difficult sites. The Fish Creek LRT bridge was the first of a short-lived design-build process for the City of Calgary. In Martin's proposal, the build part of the equation was not price competitive — a large safety margin had been added to the construction cost because the design did not use the standard pre-cast girders that have made up most of Alberta's bridges of the last twenty years.

The bridge that was built is okay; it could have been worse, but it could have been better. When, in 1980, Martin suggested that Arup open an office in Calgary, given the amount of construction work in this province since the 1960s, Arup said it would be like sending coals to Newcastle. Evidently, Canada is overrun with structural engineers. When the Alberta Transportation and Engineering Department was disbanded in the early 1990s, it released a further flood of engineers on the market. One would think that both the province and this very wealthy city would have an amazing record of engineered infrastructure, including bridges, overpasses, and flood control devices; however, it doesn't. It seems to have been crippled by an extreme financial conservatism that led to a design conservatism, so much so that when special bridges are needed, such as the pedestrian bridges over the Bow River, local engineers are bypassed. This project for the Fish Creek LRT bridge is an example of an engineering standard, local and elegant, that was unbuilt.

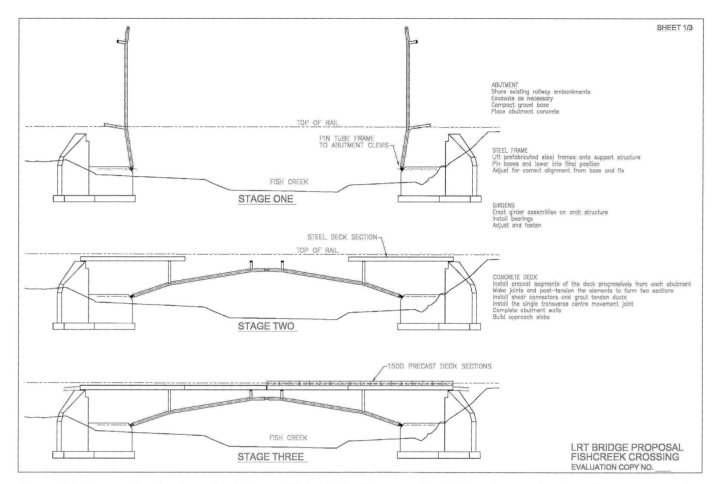

Figure 16-1. Compared to the Manu Chugh St. Patrick's footbridge (chapter 15), which is a planar surface hung from a structure that becomes a feature, Tom Martin's Fish Creek LRT bridge is a flat deck supported from underneath, so its structure is hidden. Within this proposal is also a strategy for construction. Half the structure is built on each half of the creek bed and then lowered to meet in the middle, where the arch is fastened. Precast segments of the concrete deck are added from each abutment, also meeting in the centre. This is a delicate and precise operation that does not require a lot of disruptive scaffolding and equipment in the creek itself.
Tom Martin Consultants, Calgary, Alberta.

Fish Creek LRT Bridge

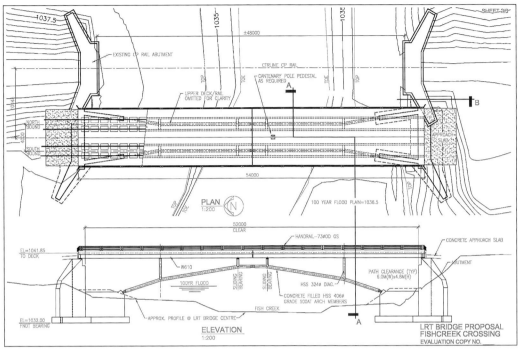

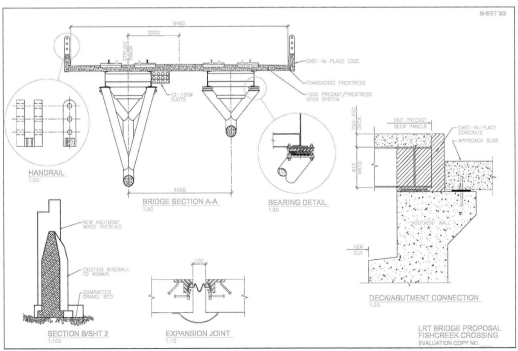

OIL AND GAS URBANISM

Chapter 17

The Clipping Files

One of the interesting things about just how few projects were proposed in Calgary that did not see the light of day is revealed in the Calgary Public Library's "buildings" clipping files. Researchers find these library clipping files full of gold dust — tiny 6pt text on yellow newsprint, a few hundred words that take one right back to 1928, or 1962, or to some other time we have all forgotten about.

Often plans for new buildings or development meet public opposition, and this sells papers, so just relying on newspapers alone would give one a very distorted view of what a city felt about its changes. Although public opinion can be effective in stopping projects, such as happened with the 1964 Bow River transportation corridor, more often it is to no avail. At the end of 1974, several City of Calgary aldermen protested the almost unilateral choice by the federal government and the mayor of the time, Rod Sykes, to put a new federal building in Chinatown. Aldermen Hartman and Petrasuk said it would "smother Chinatown" and cause "exceptional human suffering for relocated senior citizens." Other aldermen pointed out the poor transit connections and the ever-present danger of building on the Bow River flood plain.[1] Rod Sykes, the head of the land division of the Canadian Pacific Railway before officially entering into local politics, was an immensely powerful figure in Calgary and very pro-development. Chinese grandparents living in small flats in the blocks of Chinatown that were slated for urban renewal didn't stand a chance. They were relocated to two fifteen-storey slabs in east Calgary.

The federal building could have gone elsewhere, east Calgary perhaps, but Chinatown in the 1970s was seen as an obstruction to the development of the downtown core and a kind of disgrace in a city inventing

---

1   The *Calgary Herald*. December 10, 1974.

de-built Calgary, the dismantling of the old wood, brick, and sandstone, two- and three-storey city to make way for the ten-storey new world of oil and gas. Old Calgary couldn't have been saved or retained; cities do develop. It is more about how citizens feel about such development, and in Calgary regret was expressed, briefly, and then overtaken by absolute pride in the new projects. The newspapers were full of lists of buildings underway. The language is enthralled, as seen on March 14, 1956, when the *Herald* reported "Calgary's first all-glass building" at 8th Avenue and 7th Street West for Petro-Chemical Buildings, a local syndicate led by Sun Oil.

Chapter 19

9th Avenue and 4th Street Southwest

Just one major unbuilt project was found in the stack of perhaps four hundred clippings covering over a hundred years. From 1957 there is a *Calgary Herald* article, "Skyscraper Plan Rejected by City." This was a twenty-one-storey office building at 9th Avenue and 4th Street Southwest designed by Calgary architects Abugov and Sunderland, who in 1966 went on to design the tallest building west of Toronto, Edmonton's CN Tower. Calgary bylaws, however, restricted building height to twelve storeys in the downtown core. The project was proposed by Hymie Singer who had bought the site from the City of Calgary. The extended and interrelated families of Switzers, Belzburgs, and Singers — Polish immigrants to Calgary in the early 1900s — have had an important spatial influence on the cultural life of the city.

At the time, the site was occupied by the Bruce Robinson Building, a brick and sandstone-lintelled warehouse. The City of Calgary had toyed with renovating the building as an extension to the library in Central Park, two blocks away,[1] but sold it to Singer instead. The City of Calgary rejected Singer's skyscraper proposal and suggested a two-storey parking garage instead. Singer tried again to develop this site in 1971, proposing a twenty-storey hotel and conference centre, designed by Bill Milne. This, too, failed. The parking structure was built.

The reason given for not developing the site to a very high density was fear of adding to traffic congestion in the downtown area, a problem that spurred the construction of the light rail transit system, recommended in a transportation report in 1967, proposed in 1975, started in 1978, and opened in 1981. The effect of the LRT was to lift the cap on building height and floor-area ratio (used to calculate height in relation to the size of the site and site coverage).

---

1   *The Albertan*. May 25, 1957.

[94] Unbuilt Calgary

Figure 19-1. The first proposal for Alberta 75 Place shows a very clean structure, magically narrowed to a visually thin point above an atrium base. Although one can see the structural columns on the south and north sides, and the central slab that all together support the 75 storeys, it still appears as if the tower balances on a tiny pivot point. It appears to hang above the street.

Figure 19-2. The second proposal for Alberta 75 shows a much sturdier project, basically the same as the first version but more grounded. It is all in the proportions.

Figure 19-3. A detail of the base: open, glassy, many levelled, and treed on a complex site where 4th Street plunges under 9th Avenue and the railway tracks. In reality, a fearful site of much concrete and traffic.

In 1981 the Gagliardi Group, which owned Sandman Inns, proposed a seventy-five-storey hotel and office project, designed by Ron Boruk Architects, on this site, zoned for 8 FAR (the total floor area is eight times the area of the site). Alberta 75, so named to coincide with the 75th anniversary of Calgary in 1980, managed to parlay the FAR on the site to 24 to achieve 75 storeys. The first version of this project is a thin Skylon-form pinned to a chamfered atrium that was designed to both bring winter light deep into the base of the project and to break the downdraft winds that make downtown sidewalks so cold and blustery in the winter. It is an interesting formal strategy, tested at the time at the Rowan Williams Davies & Irwin wind tunnel lab in Guelph and used by them as a demonstration project, but never actually adopted in Calgary.

Approval for the first version stalled at the City of Calgary, and a second version was developed, for a shorter, faceted tower that provided twelve corner offices per floor, a distinct advantage for corporate hierarchical spatiality. Although this project did get final approval from the City of Calgary, by 1984 financing was not available and the project did not proceed. In the meantime, the four-storey concrete parking garage on 9th Avenue and 4th Street Southwest would do, and it still does.

In the Boruk proposal is a tiny vest pocket park taking up the grade change as 4th Street goes under the railway tracks. Downtown Calgary is a very tough environment today; pavement meets concrete planters, or building walls. The riverbank nature of this small piece of landscaping filling in a corner of a fully developed lot seems gracious to our eyes today, especially given what is actually on that very inhospitable site.

McIntyre Plaza, developed by Burgener Lachapelle Architects (discussed later in chapter 21), and Alberta 75 Place, developed by Ron Boruk Architects, were huge projects given to young offices that were catapulted into architectural opportunities unavailable in normal times. Booms escalate everything. Ron Boruk had only just started his own practice, as had Burgener Lachapelle. This kind of start to a career is inconceivable today.

Chapter 20

Downtown Roads

Calgary has downtown traffic problems: the streets are narrow, dating from the original CPR layout when Calgary was simply a divisional point, like Medicine Hat or Red Deer. The CPR-controlled townsite development, and CPR draftsmen laid out the road system within the confines of the Dominion Survey. The city was small until the wheat boom propelled Calgary into something larger than a way station. The present high concentration of high-rise real estate on a road pattern not that was never expected to be more than a small town began to emerge as a near-crisis by 1960, when Bill Milne proposed his novel and unusual solution to Calgary's already established downtown woes, followed by the dramatic South Bow River Parkway proposal of 1963–64. Nevertheless, when we look at some of the downtown commercial work in the 1950s, we see a fairly delicate commercial scale. These drawings are from the files of Albert Dale; street sketches show a close and busy downtown. A couple of minimalist modern office buildings stretch across small sites; sidewalks are included as a vital component of the building fronts. This is downtown urban architecture at the scale of details. Decades later, with whole block amalgamations and seventy-five-storey towers on wide plazas, architects imply details but deal mostly with building systems.

If this delicate scale was the norm in the 1950s, it offers us some background as to why Gordon Atkins in 1963 found the new urban renewal landscape at the east end of 7th Avenue so unresponsive to human habitation. He drew out the two sides of 7th Avenue that surrounded City Hall, showing institutional buildings that did not care much about sidewalk life, a condition that Calgary has struggled with ever since, first with the implementation of the +15 system and now with the proliferation of privately owned public open spaces at the base of the newest towers.

Several one-way east-west transportation corridors were established in the 1980s: 9th Avenue is one-way east, leading to 17th Avenue and Deerfoot Trail; 8th Avenue is pedestrian; 7th Avenue is where all the LRT lines converge, as anticipated by Atkins in 1963; 6th Avenue is one-way west leading to Bow and Crowchild Trails; 5th Avenue is one-way east, leading to Edmonton Trail and Memorial Drive. North-south streets mostly lead to avenue sub-corridors (an echo of Milne's 1960 proposals) and aren't major corridors until they leave the downtown core.

Figure 20-1. This is a random sketch found in the Dale files, undated and untitled, but in the same roll as the small offices (figure 20-2). It shows how intimate downtown Calgary was, even 9th Avenue. This sketch was done in front of what had been the quite beautiful modernist main post office on the southwest corner of 9th Avenue and 1st Street Southwest. We are looking at the corner of the Palliser on the right. The building on the left is gone, replaced by the plaza of the Marathon tower, built on that site.

Dale Chandler Kennedy fonds. Canadian Architectural Archives, University of Calgary. 47A/79.03, DAL ad/126.

[98] Unbuilt Calgary

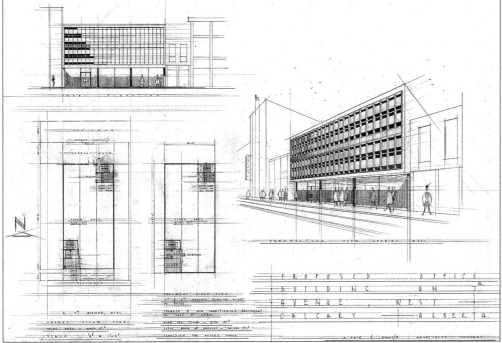

Figure 20-2. Another two proposals, again for small properties in the heart of the city core. We are now used to any new project being a minimum of half a block, and, increasingly, full blocks. There is no room for this kind of scale any more.
Dale Chandler Kennedy fonds. Canadian Architectural Archives, University of Calgary. 47A/79.03, DAL ad/115 and ad/126.

Figure 20-3. One of Atkins's objections was to the filling up of a whole block with a single occupant, such as the police station or the City Hall annex. The texture of Calgary was fine — many narrow lots that gave a liveliness of occupancy. This proposal is for 144 8th Avenue Southeast in the block that was obliterated by the Glenbow and the Convention Centre, part of the massive reworking of the old CPR landscape. The part of 8th Avenue we love is the historic fine grain of the Hudson's Bay block and the one directly east of it, where the narrow shop fronts remain. In the 1950s and the early 1960s, such fine grain was not considered just a historic sandstone reality but was available for contemporary architecture, as this project shows.

Dale Chandler Kennedy fonds. Canadian Architectural Archives, University of Calgary. 47A/79.03, DAL ad/126.

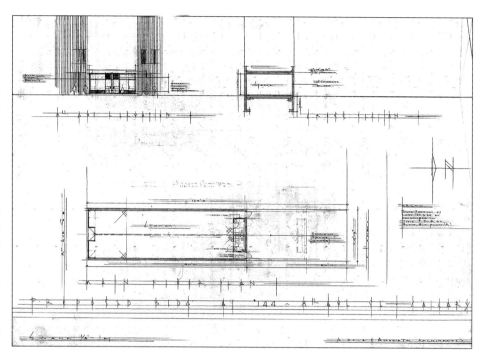

Figure 20-4. The two sides of 7th Avenue in the City Hall block, 1963. On the north side is the library, then the police station, which fills the rest of the block with a parking garage at the end. Facing is the City Hall and then a long early 1960s City Hall addition to the end of the block. It is all still there, except for the parking garage, which was removed in 2011. Atkins did not feel that this was a welcoming or significant civic landscape. Fifteen years later, the Hanen and Moriyama Civic Centre (chapter 10) plan more or less ignored this block, concentrating on remaking 8th Avenue instead.

Gordon Atkins fonds. Canadian Architectural Archives, University of Calgary. 263A/99.02, ATK A63-01.

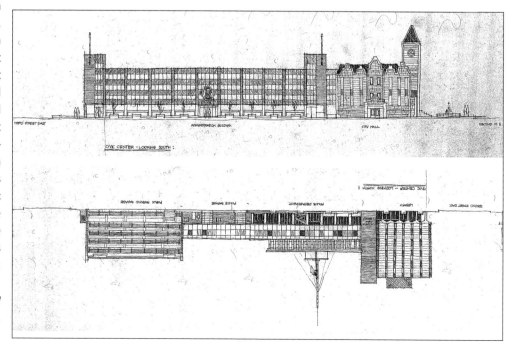

Chapter 21

7th Avenue

The quality of urban life on 7th Avenue, the LRT and bus corridor, would be much different if a couple of key projects had been built, starting with some possible configurations of the 1984 Calgary Municipal Building. The 1980 First Stage Requirement for the Architectural Competition for the Design of a Municipal Building in Calgary shows some civic intentions that were never developed. This competition was set just two years after the defeat of the 1978 Civic Centre plan, which carved out a large plaza, surrounded by large amphitheatrical masses at the east end of 8th Avenue, scaled to hold large gatherings and festivals. The full extent of the Civic Centre plan was not realized, but it did influence the setting of the brief for the new municipal building. The brief shows the cutting off of 8th Avenue, which, however, had already been cut off by the then-new LRT South line, which emerged from a tunnel at 9th Avenue and swung around in an arc to 7th Avenue to an above-ground station. There was, in the plan for the new Municipal Building, an underground LRT station at the site that became Olympic Plaza, across the street from City Hall. The old ceremonial park beside City Hall was meant to be incorporated into a ceremonial plaza that continued through the 8th Avenue axis to parking at the back of the Municipal Building. The design for the Municipal Building and the other entries that responded to the competition brief are discussed in chapter thirteen; here, we will just consider the nature of ceremonial public space, transportation systems, and civic intentions.

The original LRT plan was meant to run underneath 8th Avenue, already the main pedestrian east-west thoroughfare for downtown. However, at the time of the building of the new Municipal Building, the LRT project was $23 million over budget, and the underground route, which would have been very disruptive and expensive to build, was abandoned. The only trace of this underground route is an abandoned section of tunnel under the Municipal Building.

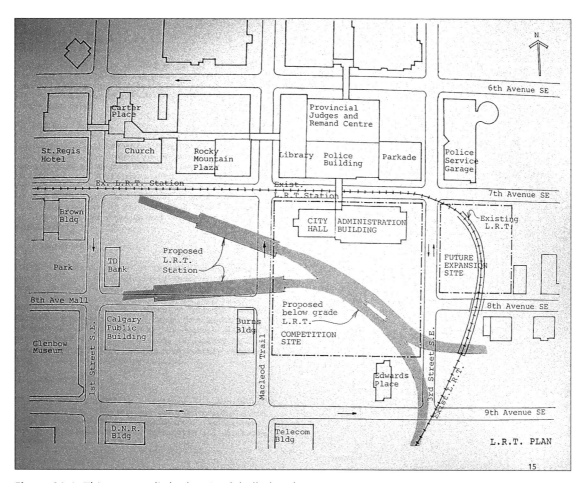

Figure 21-1. This scrappy little drawing labelled with a typewriter was part of the competition brief for the Municipal Building (see chapter 12). It shows the proposed below-grade LRT along with the newly opened southwest LRT line that emerges from a long tunnel that starts at the Stampede station on 12th Avenue Southeast. The northeast line joins the southwest line on 7th Avenue now but at the time of the competition had not yet been built. The proposed underground station includes a connection to the northeast line. Let us suppose the underground line had been built and extended throughout the length of downtown, leaving 7th Avenue to be something other than a traffic corridor dominated by raised platforms and concrete-crowded sidewalks. Just a thought.
Calgary Municipal Building Competition Brief, City of Calgary, 1981.

The decision to make 7th Avenue a transportation corridor for light rail transit, buses, and police vehicles harkens back to Gordon Atkins' scheme of 1963. In the late 1970s, before 7th Avenue became an LRT transit corridor, sidewalks were often busy in the early evening — cars cruised, theatres were open, there were late shopping hours, and people could be seen. This kind of Friday night activity eventually moved to the malls, but the downtown core at night was still an important public place in the late 1970s. A couple of years later, by the early 1980s, there was a lament that the downtown core was empty after 6:00 p.m. Movie theatres and coffee shops were no longer sustainable, although more adult entertainment was; tourists had slim pickings in the evenings, and this was perhaps the beginning of Calgary's big city image problem.

Had the LRT line gone underground through the city core, and normal street relations of buses, cars, and parking been maintained, parts of 7th Avenue might not be the no-man's land that they are today. The theory that one can have a narrow street full of a variety of public transit forms, but no cars, has proven to be fairly deadly in terms of urban friendliness. The sidewalks are squeezed by a street wall of either the inhospitable bases of office towers, or on some blocks, downmarket pawn shops and cheap eateries. It is all too narrow and too inconsistent.

At the peak of the second oil boom, which was about to come crashing down for a number of reasons — not least a worldwide recession — we find Burgener Lachapelle's project, McIntyre Plaza, on a site that achieved an unprecedented and still unmatched density for development. This, too, is a project that remains unbuilt, not because it would have led to congestion, which it would have, but because the market briefly fell out of love with downtown development in Calgary.

This project also shows something of the heady atmosphere of Calgary's development boom in the very early 1980s, considering that a very young architecture firm, Burgener Lachapelle Architects, after coming second in a different Cascade Development Corporation project for the development of the bus barns site, was given such a large project by Cascade. It was the highest density reclassification application in Calgary's history, 25.6 FAR, which was approved by the City of Calgary and which the site still holds.

In the 1984 book *Calgary Architecture: The Boom Years, 1972–1982* by Pierre Guimond and Brian Sinclair, a classic of second-oil-boom Calgary architectural history, there is a chapter near the back of unbuilt projects. With the hindsight of thirty-odd years, they clearly form a distinct office-tower typology: curtain-wall towers, on plazas, many by Toronto's Webb Zerafa Menkes Housden Architects. Within this typology, both built and unbuilt projects achieved their staggering density and height through the inclusion of a number of public amenities, meant to ameliorate the effects of over-building the site. McIntyre Plaza's height amelioration included a very large public plaza on the LRT corridor, and it is this, rather than the distinctive curvature on the towers' corners, that registers today as a loss to the spatial quality of the downtown core. The project gives us some hint of how 7th Avenue might have been opened up to become the vital urban thoroughfare of a revitalized city as a series of open plazas, linked like pearls on the strand of the light rail transit line.

Figure 21-2. If you go back to the original CPR block layout (figure 0-3), we find that 7th Avenue was originally named McIntyre Avenue. Duncan McIntyre was the president of the Canada Central Railway in 1880, just as it was taken over by the CPR. McIntyre was made vice-president of the CPR, leaving in 1884 over differences with George Stephen, the CPR's first president and banker. The irony is they were forever aligned in Calgary's street system.
David Lachapelle Architects.

To treat an above-ground light rail transit stop as if it was merely a utility, or simply something like a bus stop, invisible on the sidewalk but for a sign, ignores the potential for a transit line to knit a city together in a kind of public spatiality that goes beyond the street network. McIntyre plaza captures the original enthusiasm for each LRT stop to be an event in a public open space. Burgener Lachapelle's project was a kind of commercial tower architecture that dissolved in refracted and mirrored light, disappearing in reflected skies. All attention would be on the plaza that started at ground level on 7th Avenue, stepped up to the +15 and +30 levels mid-block, and then back down to 8th Avenue. Its success would have depended on a lot of pedestrians, supposedly delivered to the downtown core from far-flung suburbia and exurbia by the LRT.

One tall building problem that has emerged recently with an increased violence of weather is the problem of glass panels breaking off the curtain walls in wind storms. Rounding the corners of towers, seen in McIntyre Plaza, along the principles of the aileron redirects winds rather than having them, so much stronger at the 30th floor, slamming the wall head on. Neither Boruk's Alberta 75 project, which brilliantly managed tall building downdrafts, nor Burgener Lachapelle's McIntyre Plaza's management of wind force damage became the standard practice they ought to have.

All sorts of innovations were thrown away with the plans of the unbuilt projects of the early 1980s. Raising extreme FARS by offering public amenities occurred over a relatively brief period in the late 1970s and early 1980s. This was when the vision of Calgary was held as much in its proposed public civic spaces, such as the 1978 Civic Centre, or McIntyre Plaza, as it was in the assemblage of a whole city of mirrored curtain wall towers. It is curious, looking back, how compressed this era was.

OUTSIDE THE DOWNTOWN CORE

Chapter 22

The 1910 Aerial Drawing

A view of Calgary drawn in 1910 shows something of its topography and how a city of ten thousand occupied a flood plain between two rivers and a few escarpments. Future street grids are sketched to the east of the Bow River, some in the northwest and others lightly indicated in the southwest. This was the Calgary that Thomas Mawson saw when he came through in 1911 at the tail end of the wheat boom that had spurred the building of this small city. We must always keep this in mind when looking at Mawson's quite grandiose plan.

Let's consider the making of this 1910 bird's-eye view. The first airplane flight in Alberta was in 1911, and although the brother of Louis Blériot, André Blériot, immigrated to Alberta in 1901 and homesteaded at Munson, he wasn't the flyer, and there is no record of Louis visiting Canada. Hot air balloons had been invented in the late eighteenth century, but balloons with onboard heat sources weren't developed until the 1950s. There could have been a hot air balloon in Calgary in 1910, but if so, no one has made mention of such a remarkable event.

No, this map is a drawing of imagination, taken from topographic surveys, observation, and views from the street. Interestingly, not a lot has changed: downtown is still where it was, tall and dense, flanking the tracks; Fort Calgary is squeezed between the Elbow and the Bow Rivers, and a train station; Edmonton Trail is much as it was then, as is 9th Avenue East, leading out of the city. The north is squeezed between two hills, both empty. Other maps of the time show these as large reserves. The one on the east side became an airport, and much, much later, the west side became the Institute of Technology and University of Calgary corridor. On this map there is a location for a university, a nice classical building is scratched in at the west end of 17th Avenue.

[108] Unbuilt Calgary

Figure 22-1. The dating of this drawing is, evidently, an educated guess. It appears to be around 1910 and shows, quite accurately, the basic topography of Calgary, including the dramatic escarpments, foothills, and valleys, and the potential for vast subdivisions stretching east where the land is the most flat. South Morley Trail appears to be what is now Richmond Road, cutting diagonally across the southwest, and North Morely Trail is probably Crowchild Trail today. Nose Hill dominates the northern skyline, and Nose Creek provided a protected channel for a rail line. That there was a red light district where Nose Creek meets the Bow River — must have been railway-related. Hubalta is a Grand Trunk siding at 17th Avenue and what is now 58th Street Southeast, later a little town, then the site of the Monarch Refinery, built in 1939, which became Hub Oil, which recycled used oil. It exploded and burned down in 1999. Remediation of the land began in 2001 and continues still, including a 1.2-metre clay cap over the site and extensive groundwater monitoring.

H.M. Burton, "Bird's Eye View of Calgary, 1910." Calgary Engraving Company.

Chapter 23

University of Calgary

The story of the University of Calgary is quite complex and quite long. The Calgary Normal School for training teachers was established in Calgary in 1905; in 1906 Edmonton was awarded a provincially funded university, which became the University of Alberta. The Calgary Normal School built its own building in 1906, and a separate institution, Calgary College, was founded in 1911, occupying space at the library in Central Park. One of the Calgary College board members, W.J. Tregillis, donated one hundred and sixty acres, a quarter section, in Rosscarrock on 17th Avenue west for a future university, which clearly he expected Calgary College to become. In 1914 the City of Calgary gave a grant for the construction of the new Calgary College building, designed by the splendidly named Howard Burlingham Dunington-Grubb and architects Hodgson, Bates, and Beattie, so that it could move out of the library.

However, when Calgary College applied to the province for degree-granting power, its request was turned down, and the Province of Alberta suggested that Calgary be the site for technology institute instead. Calgary College soon closed, its ambitions to be a university thwarted, another casualty of the collapse of Calgary's real estate boom, which had plunged the city into a deep recession. The Normal School ploughed on until it joined the Provincial Institute of Technology and Art in 1922. After the Second World War, the Normal School became the Calgary branch of the University of Alberta's Faculty of Education.

The land that had been donated in 1912 by the Calgary College board member for a university in Rosscarrock and was held in trust by the city was exchanged in 1950 for the present University of Calgary site on Crowchild Trail, then the highway to Banff. However, the new university was still a branch of the University of Alberta, which sold much of the newly exchanged land, thinking that the University of Alberta in Calgary would always remain a small branch. However, the University of Alberta in Calgary continued to expand its courses in response to local needs, and in 1959 the building of a new campus was started. In 1960 the Arts and Education Building (now named the Administration Building) and the Science and Engineering Building (now named Science A) were opened. They still stand — elegant, modest, postwar modern buildings, generous of space and windows. The Library Block followed in 1963, another strong building. These early University of Alberta in Calgary buildings are exemplary, but are crowded and overshadowed by subsequent campus development that was not exemplary at all.

1958 Plan

On October 1958 the University of Alberta in Calgary was announced in the *Calgary Herald* with a photograph of the premier of Alberta, the minister and deputy minister of Public Works Alberta, the chief architect of Public Works, and the project architect. Misnamed as Sigmund in the *Calgary Herald* caption, Sigfried Dietze was the architect who would have done the layout of the new campus. He was a German immigrant who studied architecture at the University of British Columbia, graduating in 1958 at the age of twenty-eight. This is his layout, perhaps his first project, showing a very modest modernism.

The 1959 Department of Public Works drawing derived from the presentation model and plans shows a central square sectioned into pools, plazas, and open parkland. Grouped around the central square are the science, arts, visual arts, physical education, and the student union buildings. One enters the university through a combination of botanical garden and parking; the entry drive becomes a main mall with everything related to it. UBC, where Dietze had just come from, is organized into malls — his plan for the new university clearly borrows from it. Future secondary malls are indicated at right angles to the main mall, leading to further clusters such as an education complex, dormitories flanking playing fields (again, found at UBC), and future faculties as yet unnamed. As a design, it is conservative, measured, formal, and spatially balanced with a sense of order completely absent in the next long-range plan, proposed a decade later. There appears to be some conceptual design conflict between Public Works Alberta's view of what a campus should be and the newly liberated University of Calgary, which, from its long-range plan, seems to have thrown out any kind of orthogonal relationship between buildings and faculties.

Figure 23-1. Arthur Arnold, deputy minister of Public Works; Hon. E.C. Manning, premier; Hon. A.R. Patrick, minister of Economic Affairs; Hon. James Hartley, minister of Public Works; Sigfried Dietze, project architect; and H.A. Henderson, chief architect, Department of Public Works, examining a scale model of the proposed University of Alberta in Calgary campus, October 1958.

Calgary Herald fonds, University Archives, University of Calgary. 82.010-1.07.

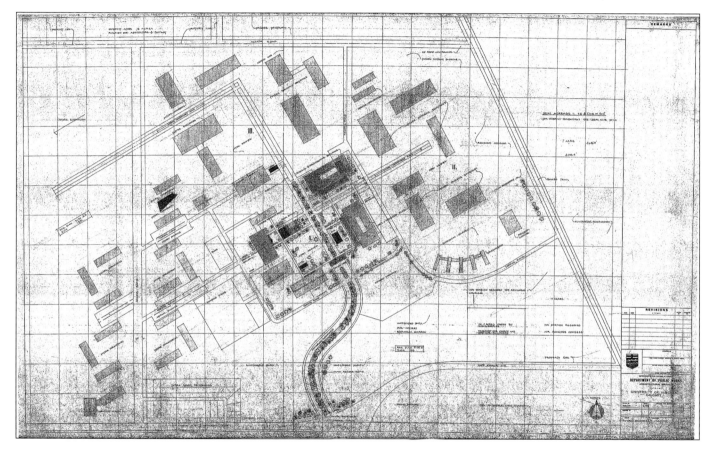

Figure 23-2. A more developed layout by the Department of Public Works, Government of Alberta, indicates the interweaving of buildings, tall and low, with parades, malls, squares, and pathways, orthogonal in plan, but in section and elevation, a composition of point blocks and spreading horizontal platforms. Unsentimental, yet intimate; mathematical, leavened by landscape.

Canadian Architectural Archives, University of Calgary.

Long-Range Development Plan

It is very difficult to discern any kind of recognizable or conventional order in the University of Calgary long-range future development plan (figure 23-3) published in 1965. In the intervening years, Calgary — citizens and city alike — had lobbied hard to achieve autonomy from the University of Alberta and did so in 1966. This long-range plan can be seen as a declaration of decolonization, with all the hubris that seems to have accompanied it.

Distracting, in this drawing, are the many pathway systems and what appears to be parking buildings, the large squares on the south side, which are at least three storeys tall. The southeast corner, the little bars in the plan, are residences: free-standing blocks in fields of green that echo the ground-breaking (for Calgary) mini-Ville Radieuse Spruce Cliff Apartments of 1954, a bit south across the Bow River. Further residences in the southwest corner show as two star-shaped towers sharing an octagonal dining hall; these towers were eventually built. Student health services are next door, while a physical education building and a sports track are directly north. Residential fabric on the outskirts of the campus reflects the postwar expansion of Calgary itself — the downtown core and its unfashionable inner city neighbourhoods were increasingly surrounded with suburban development in ever-widening rings. The University of Calgary campus was located in this suburban ring and replicated suburbanism as a planning ethos..

Social sciences, the library, and a dining hall are at the geographic centre of this plan. The library building (10) is not on axis with the social sciences building (4) although it is connected to an administration building (9). The student centre (11) is detached from this central complex, clearly pulling away from it, and neither residential living nor student activities are integrated with learning. There is a ring road, which leaves the centre of the campus car-free. The buildings that had been built in 1958 are on this plan, but most of the buildings and faculties in this long-range plan differ from what was subsequently built. However, the basic view of a university as a series of silos connected only on the ground plane by wandering paths and trees did direct University of Calgary development. Unanticipated in 1968 is the Haskayne School of Business, located today on the south edge of the campus, pointing downtown, away from the campus itself. Its affiliation to the business environment of Calgary is made very clear. Nor was the Engineering and Innovative Technologies complex on the northwest corner of the campus forecast as quite the architectural mini-campus that it has become. The University of Calgary has moved in a different direction from its historical roots in education and the liberal arts toward business and engineering, more in line with the twenty-first century industrial base of Calgary itself.

Had the university been built on its original site in Rosscarrock, it would have still been suburban, so it wouldn't have had a drastically different effect on the university's relationship with the city core. It might have had some effect on surrounding development; however, if we look at the small neighbourhoods that pre-dated the present location of the University of Calgary, proximity to such an institution isn't a guarantee of anything.

As a footnote to the suburban location of the University of Calgary, in the 1958 plan, a future civic stadium was indicated directly south of the university grounds, which did become McMahon Stadium, built in 1960 with money donated by the McMahon brothers

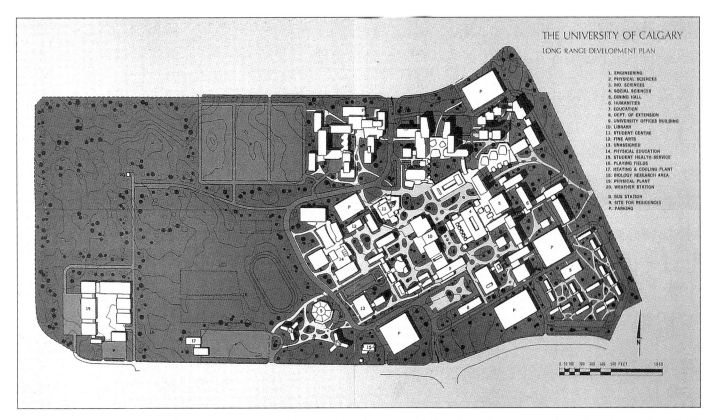

Figure 23-3. By 1968 we find that modernist rigour is gone. There is no overall clear formal strategy; rather, there is a series of individual quarters, each with its own logic. This was 1968, the year of student revolt around the world. It is difficult to discern a centre here, so carved and interrupted is the open space it effectively prevents assembly. Not that Calgary would ever have been a hotbed of socialist student movements — it has never been that kind of city, but even if it had, the University of Calgary, in its partly rural, mostly suburban location, would defuse and disperse crowds through sheer lack of intensity.
Courtesy of the Calgary Public Library, Community Heritage and Family History Collection.

to the McMahon Stadium Society on city property. McMahon Stadium replaced the 1905 Mewata Stadium at the Mewata Armouries in west downtown as well as many of the activities at the Buffalo Stadium in the heart of downtown. Later, the University of Calgary acquired McMahon in 1985 in a land exchange with the City of Calgary. This was a powerful move, to begin to decentralize sports sites that had previously contributed to the intensity of the downtown core. It shows however, what a bold and contrarian decision it was in 1984 to build the Saddledome at the Stampede Grounds, rather than in a wider, more open, less expensive suburban location

Chapter 24

Shouldice/Montgomery

Let us go back to our 1910 aerial, where the proposed university sits opposite Shouldice, across the Bow River. The story of Shouldice is replicated all around the city and would have been similar in Rosscarrock, not in exact details but in the general development from agricultural land to Calgary neighbourhood. In 1906, James Shouldice bought a piece of land to farm. By 1910 his farm was rezoned, he had given one hundred acres to the City of Calgary for a park, and he had divided the rest into small lots, which became Shouldice Terrace. Then, the real estate boom ended, the First World War started, and development ceased. To avoid confusion with the town of Shouldice, Alberta, Shouldice Terrace was renamed Montgomery in 1943 after General Montgomery, who defeated Rommel at El Alamein in May 1943. Shouldice/Montgomery was a separate town until 1963, when it was annexed to Calgary, and today as Montgomery it is almost a hidden community.

One of the effects of a resource boom and consequent real estate boom can be seen in a number of places in Calgary where farmland has been turned over to development — under boom circumstances, there is more money to be made by subdividing one's quarter section than there is in farming it, or ranching on it. This happened in Spruce Cliff, once the location of Lowry's Gardens, a large market garden and greenhouse serving the city. A 1905 map shows the section lines and farmhouses; the next map, in 1910, shows the whole plateau divided into thousands of tiny lots. Most of these lots defaulted to the City of Calgary in lieu of taxes during the depression of the 1930s, allowing the City of Calgary to assemble a large tract of land for postwar development in 1953, when the 118-unit Spruce Cliff apartments were built, becoming the first modern apartment complex in Calgary.

Figure 24-1. This is the section of the 1910 Burton aerial drawing of Calgary (figure 22-1, page 108) that covers west downtown from Mewata Park to Shouldice Terrace. Morley Trail is now the path of Crowchild Trail, and the university is shown in Rosscarrock at the end of 17th Avenue Southwest.

H.M. Burton, "Bird's Eye View of Calgary, 1910." Calgary Engraving Company.

A similar process occurred in Shouldice. The complex topography of river bench and low escarpment was perhaps not suited to cattle, and its clay soil — for it is directly across the Bow River from Brickburn, a clay quarry that produced early Calgary's red bricks — was perhaps not suited to crops. The houses built after the property was subdivided are small, and Montgomery isn't considered to be a particularly wealthy spot despite its excellent location by the Bow River. Montgomery's proximity to the University of Calgary also should have made it a desirable location, but in the 1960s, it suffered by not being a new, fresh postwar subdivision such as Varsity Estates, which directly abuts the university. Montgomery does not have a significant main street to provide focus; it is a small and humble anteroom to Bowness, also a separate town until the 1960s and which has a strong, cohesive sense of itself.

What is unbuilt here is not the physical fabric — that exists. Rather, it is unfulfilled. Montgomery's strategic position should have made it a more important place. Because of the dramatic change in elevation from the low, flat Bow River Valley and the University of Calgary, Foothills Hospital and the Alberta Children's Hospital spread out on the plateau above, and because of the conjunction of several major traffic arteries — Memorial Drive, the Trans-Canada Highway and Shaganappi Trail — Montgomery finds itself squeezed between the base of an escarpment and Memorial Drive, cut off from the river, from Bowness and Shouldice Park. One would think that the proximity to the university and the hospitals would be an advantage to Montgomery's rediscovery and consequent gentrification, but it hasn't been so. Montgomery remains a relatively small community, spirited but often overlooked.

In 1983, during a recession following the development of a national energy policy that caused many foreign oil companies to pull out of the tar sands (as they were then called) of northern Alberta, Calgary experienced a small building boom because of the coming 1988 Winter Olympics. This small Olympic-fuelled boom included a housing project for Shouldice, between the Trans-Canada Highway and the Bow River.

Chapter 25
River's Edge Village

When a city is awarded an Olympic Games, it is an opportunity to build some major amenities and new infrastructure. There are the sports facilities of course, the glamour-end of Olympic architecture, but there is also substantial housing added to the city for both the athletes' village and the press. When such housing is contentious, as it was for the 1992 Olympics in Barcelona, the 2008 Olympics in Beijing, and the 2010 Winter Olympics in Vancouver, it is because such large housing projects are often an excuse for some necessary urban renewal, which often results in poor people displaced, land appropriated and bad feeling amongst the socially vulnerable Olympic fever seems to impel civic administrations to be decisive in a way they rarely can be normally.

In Calgary a new hockey arena was put in the Stampede grounds, a speed skating oval went on the University of Calgary campus, opening ceremonies were held in the existing McMahon Stadium adjacent to the university grounds, and medals were awarded at Olympic Plaza, downtown across the street from City Hall. Ski jump towers and the tracks for luge and skeleton were built at Calgary Olympic Park on the Paskapoo slopes, where a small ski hill that had been built in the 1960s was much amplified for the 1988 Winter Olympics. The rest of the Olympic venues were located in the mountains of the Kananaskis. Other than the Saddledome and Olympic Plaza, the traffic and events took place in the northwest quarter of Calgary, springing off west along the Trans-Canada Highway to the mountains.

A call went out in 1985 for proposals for Olympic Media Housing for five thousand media personnel. Applicants had to have either the site in hand or an option on a site, any expropriations dealt with, a construction company, the architects, a development company, a quantity surveyor, and financing, all with track records in residential housing development. Townscape Properties proposed a twenty-six-acre site on the Bow River, a tranche of land flanked by Shouldice Athletic Park, which in turn is bounded by the Trans-Canada Highway. Across the highway is a nearby shopping centre, up the hill is Foothills Hospital, and beyond that, the University of Calgary. This location was absolutely ideal, a key position perhaps a mile from Calgary Olympic Park, well-accessed, secure, and almost incidentally, a very beautiful site. Townscape owned the site and had been given a $20 million mortgage for development. Post-Olympic use was ensured — close to the university and a series of major medical facilities, the rental market, always under-supplied, would be a cinch.

The site was surprisingly rural, with fields, fence lines, hedgerows, and barns, with a rugby field at one end and a trailer park at the other on the Bow River. This was surely the most outstanding trailer park site, given that, in the city, hardly any river's-edge land is private.

The layout of the project framed a canal and lagoon system, fed by the Bow River, which would be both a summer and a winter amenity. There were a variety of apartment and townhouse units and a central clubhouse/plaza with sports and fitness facilities. It wasn't an inexpensive-looking short-term project but rather a distinctive model for medium to high density residential enclaves. Would the canals and lagoons have been part of some sort of flood-control mechanism on the Bow River floodplain?

Figure 25-1. A wide bend in the Bow River, downtown in the distance on the left. The Trans-Canada Highway wraps the extreme left of this aerial photograph, taken in 1985. Shouldice Park, its sports fields, and Gordon Atkins's beautiful, buried changing rooms are in the wedge between the highway and the old country road that bisects the flats. Across the river, one can see the CPR tracks following the Bow River into Calgary. It is an astounding piece of development property.
Dan Jenkins Architects.

Figure 25-2. The project shows a most un-Albertan density, previously accorded CMHC lower income townhouse projects. The difference here is in the landscaping, the architecture, and the use of water, all of which signal a village, rather than a housing complex.
Dan Jenkins Architects.

Figure 25-3. What is an inlet in the summer becomes a rink in the winter — a dramatic change from even contemporary shopping centres, thirty years later, that adopt the village square model, but where this centre would be full of parked cars.
Dan Jenkins Architects.

The proposal doesn't raise this issue. But even without the canals and lagoons, the planning is intimate and collegial; each cluster of units is sized to provide an identity of place. It would have enclosed Shouldice Park's west edge, giving it more shape and clarity.

This project didn't happen. The Olympic media housing was built by ATCO adjacent to Mount Royal College, as it was then on ATCO-owned land in the southwest quadrant of the city, quite a long way from Calgary Olympic Park. Its post-Olympic use is largely as student rental accommodation for Mount Royal University.

In an interesting loop of influence, Dan Jenkins, the architect for River's Edge Village, anticipated the kind of New Urbanism sensibility he later brought to Canada Lands' redevelopment of Currie Barracks. Mount Royal University was built on the old RCAF airstrip adjacent to Currie Barracks. With the decommissioning of Currie Barracks and Camp Sarcee in 1996, the army housing — the PMQs dating from the mid-1950s, were surplus to requirements and were moved around, densified, and redeveloped as Garrison Woods and Garrison Green on a New Urbanism model. As with most serious New Urbanism projects meant to have a mixed-income population, the developments are so picturesque and the variety of unit types is so accommodating that they quickly become the preserve of middle- to upper-income professionals.

This has happened in Garrison Woods and would have happened to River's Edge Village. It would have redefined the ambiguous nature of Montgomery and Bowness. The area at the foot of the escarpment underneath Foothills Hospital actually contains a wide mix of people and house types; it has been immune to the destructive force of being trendy and so retains much of its original housing stock. The building up of the river bank and the sharing of Shouldice Park would have consolidated the whole area into a stronger entity than it now appears to be. The location is powerful, advantageous in many ways; Shouldice, Montgomery, and Bowness together are the de facto west entrance to Calgary and could have signalled something more sophisticated about Calgary than the twenty miles of sprawl that incoming travellers on the highway must witness.

The other thing that is interesting about River's Edge Village is the way it treats the river. The actual edge is fractalized, extending into the land, rather than being armoured, rip-rapped and buttressed as is the Bow River in the downtown core. This project introduces something that acts almost as an oxbow, proving a slower backwater stream to the rushing, heroic Bow River. If we look at the small islands downstream — Prince's Island, St. George's and St. Patrick's Islands — they are separated from the main bank in just this way. The channel that forms Prince's Island itself was dredged by the Eau Claire Lumber Company in the 1880s and dammed at its east end by a hydroelectric power plant; the other islands result from natural channels in the width of the Bow and were long used as campsites. A closer example is Bowness Park, another Bow River island separated from the river bank by what has always been known as the lagoon, a park and a winter skating rink since 1911. These quiet backwater channels have been used in Calgary for a long time, and were taken up by the River's Edge Village proposal, but through a complex chain of circumstance, politics, influence, and expediency were not developed.

Chapter 26

OLYMPIC ARCHES

In the run-up to the 1988 Winter Olympics, an invited competition was held for an Olympic arch that would encapsulate the meaning of the Olympic movement to Calgary. One of the proposals was by Barry Johns, an Edmonton architect, who looked at the combination of sun and wind, prairie and mountains, climate and weather such as the foehn wind on the eastern slopes of the Rockies that produces a cloud formation, locally called a chinook arch. In Johns' project, a tower leans into the wind, a sundog (a lighting gantry) wraps it, and upthrust diagonals of the Rocky Mountains anchor it. It is a most un-literal arch in traditional architectural terms, but is very literal in its portrayal of the conditions in Calgary that produce a chinook arch. It also speaks to the fragility of something as complex as a city in the face of the environment: the leaning tower is all of Calgary's towers, whipped by the wind.

[122] Unbuilt Calgary

Figure 26-1. This project has several historic echoes in the leaning tower made of scaffold. The clearest is the constructivist Lenin Tribune tower designed by el Lissitzky in 1924. Then, there is OMA's Boompjes observation tower of 1980 in Rotterdam. This was a high-rise collection of several buildings in which various sections tilt out of line, fracturing the mass of the whole. A scaffold tower stood as an outlier, fragile and yet monumental, an homage to el Lissitzky. The pile of mountains too has strong reminders of béton brut forms, the most powerful local example being the original Calgary Centennial Planetarium building at Mewata by Jack Long, built between 1964 and 1966.

Barry Johns Architects Ltd.

Chapter 27

Happy Valley

Happy Valley in the 1960s was an area in the northwest part of the city, and west of Montogomer and Bowness, with a much different history. Although the area, now known as Valley Ridge, appears to be much like any new subdivision, it has a most exuberant past with a most surprising unbuilt project.

In 1965 the Calgary Sports Car Club proposed an auto track at Happy Valley to the Calgary Tourist and Convention Association. Calgary, due to the opening of the Trans-Canada Highway in 1962, had an increasing flow of visitors to the city. At this time, special events that garnered national publicity were limited to the Stampede. The Calgary Tourist and Convention Association had announced its goal of four major events for Calgary, one for each season: a Winter Carnival was scheduled for 1966, and the Stampede always took place in July — what was needed were events for the spring and fall. In Canada, in the mid-1960s, only Mossport, in Ontario, had a racetrack built to international racing regulations, and the Sports Car Club felt that Calgary was ideal for such a track in the west. Doug Johnson of the tourist association agreed, foreseeing "favourable national and international publicity."

Sports car racing boomed on the prairies in the 1950s and 1960s, and this had much to do with the dozens of small airfields that had been built as Second World War pilot-training sites under the British Commonwealth Air Training Plan. After the end of the war, most airfields were decommissioned and some were privatized, but others were used by local sports car clubs with tracks laid out on the pavement. The Calgary Sports Car Club held its first race at Airdrie Airport in 1954, and it also used Pearce, De Winton, Fort Macleod, Claresholm, and Shepard. Within the city, it used Lincoln Park Fields briefly, although it had been amalgamated with Currie Barracks, staying active until 1964 when the property was turned over to the City of Calgary and the Province of Alberta. The Calgary Sports Car Club held races there as early as 1958. In 1962 it moved its events to Fort MacLeod Airport, and Lincoln Park eventually had Mount Royal College built upon it.

Edmonton shared a similarly itinerant sports car club history until the Edmonton Speedway opened in 1968. Before it closed in 1982, it had attracted the Can Am series, Continental Formula A and Pro Atlantic races. Calgary continued to use various airport tracks until 1985 and the opening of Race City Speedway, not far from Shepard Airport, also originally a relief BCATP airport supporting Lincoln Park, and which held its first spectator race in August 1958. Clearly, for both Calgary and Edmonton there was a desire to capitalize on the lucrative racing circuit with a purpose-built speedway.

The quality of the track layouts, the facilities, and the diversity of events were design factors; whether or not spectators were safe at these race meets was also important. Prairie airfields were flat, the race tracks were flat, and any spectating was done from stands and bleachers, or on the ground where visibility was poor and safety perilous. The Happy Valley proposal, first made in 1965, was for a plot of land with a 125-foot elevation change, which acted as a natural amphitheatre for safe viewing. It laid out a three-quarter-mile oval, a three-quarter-mile drag strip, and a 2.1-mile racing circuit, plus pit and support facilities. The distances and track types are roughly equal to Edmonton's International Speedway, planned at the same time.

Originally, Happy Valley, which opened in 1961, was a family amusement area and campsite. A Calgary businessman, Ernie Lutz, bought a large tract of land the Paskapoo Slopes, a long rippling line of hills and valleys that run down from the Springbank plateau to the Bow River. Happy Valley was one of the small valleys within the greater valley of the Bow River. This is an ancient site, occupied since the retreat of the Laurentide ice sheet ten thousand years ago, which left a large lake in its wake. The area is littered with archeological evidence of habitation — tipi rings, stone tool workshops, and bison kill sites. When Ernie Lutz bought his tract, the land was six miles west of the city limits. Lutz sold his ready-mix concrete operations and embarked on building the "Disneyland of Canada."

Coincidentally, the route of the Trans-Canada Highway was laid through the middle of the Paskapoo Slopes, delivering postwar families and their baby boom children directly to Happy Valley. The completion of the Trans-Canada Highway, meant to be finished by 1956, had been held up in Alberta by a dispute over routing the highway through the Stoney Reserve at Morley. This was resolved in late 1957, and the highway finally finished in 1959, which is when Lutz made his purchase of adjacent land. By 1964, traffic on this stretch of highway was 4,500–7,000 vehicles on a normal day and 17,000 on weekends — in other words, given the population of Calgary at 300,000, very high.

Happy Valley opened with an Olympic-sized fifty-metre indoor swimming pool, a nine-hole par three golf course, a driving range, mini-golf, a carousel, trampolines, and go-carts — a family holiday heaven (see figure 27-3). Lutz developed the Paskapoo ski hill, now part of Canada Olympic Park. By 1962 it had night skiing, snow makers, two two-hundred-foot-high runs, a rope tow, and a Poma lift. In 1965 Lutz approached the Calgary Sports Car Club with a proposal for an auto track complex that included a drag strip, an oval, and a two-mile circuit (figure 27-1). Together, a plan was made, which the Sports Car Club pitched to the Tourist and Convention Association, who pitched it to the City of Calgary. The project didn't happen.

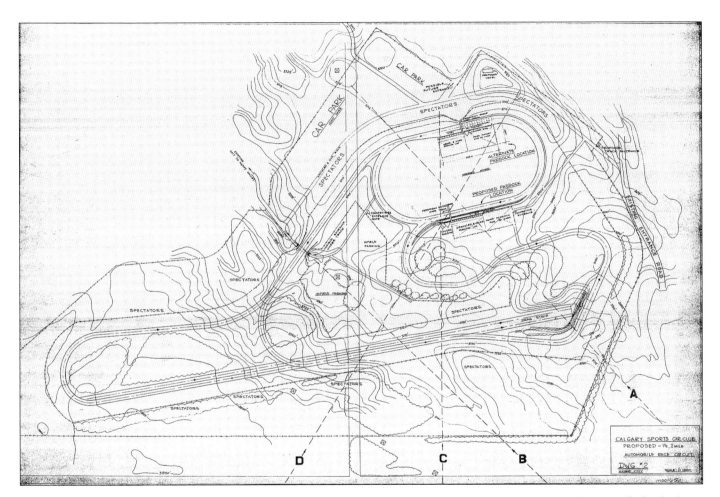

Figure 27-1. Not only did the rolling topography of this site at Happy Valley provide an interesting track with naturally banked corners, abrupt changes in grade, and lots to negotiate, but it also gave many and diverse opportunities for spectators to oversee the track and be close to the action while protected from it.

City of Calgary Corporate Records.

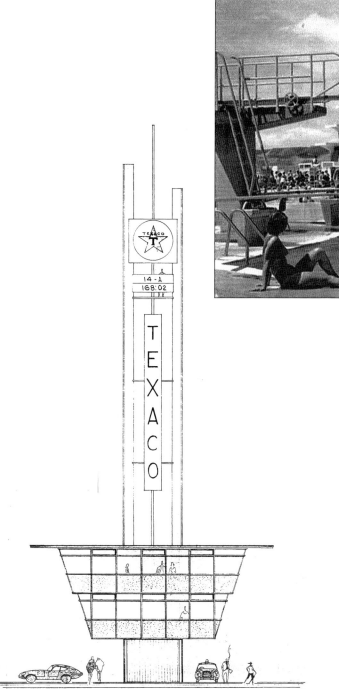

Figure 27-3. Lest one think that Happy Valley was a small project, this postcard at its zenith shows otherwise. It could be any resort, but for the foothills in the distance.

Figure 27-2. This is a nice little example of early 1960s modernism: everything is very thin, the glass is wide, and the tower stretches. Texaco had clearly backed the project in theory, although the name doesn't appear in any of the correspondence, just in this drawing. The jaunty figures at the base of the tower and their natty sports cars seem to say, "It's a sophisticated world we have here, out in Happy Valley."
City of Calgary Corporate Records.

In a 1966 article in the *Calgary Herald*, it is noted that the project was turned down by the Department of Highways, as it feared congestion on the Trans-Canada Highway, although the plan had been approved by the Calgary Regional Planning Commission and the Municipal District of Rockyview. Despite this support, the City of Calgary refused to annex Happy Valley as part of the city and the project foundered.

Lutz became ill in 1967 and sold Happy Valley to a Hollywood syndicate for $1.8 million. It wasn't maintained, fell into disrepair, and was offered to the City of Calgary in 1970, which turned it down because it was too far away (although it is advertised today as fifteen minutes to downtown); it was sold again in 1974 to a different Los Angeles–based syndicate. A group called the Friends of Happy Valley tried to raise $3.5 million to buy it back for Calgary, but couldn't. Two years later, Calgarian Bob Allen bought Happy Valley for $4 million and built an eighteen-hole golf course with a trout pond on it. Then, in 1979, Tri-Media bought the land to develop a Hollywood North complex of studios and sound stages, recording studios, industrial and commercial support, a residential community, and two more golf courses. Tri-Media later petitioned the city to annex the area, and in 1981 it did. The Hollywood North development plan failed with the 1982 economic crash. Happy Valley land reverted to receivers, and in 1989 it was bought by a development group that has built housing under the Valley Ridge Area Structure Plan. Valley Ridge is simply one of Calgary's new communities on its western flank, with Happy Valley's charismatic, entrepreneurial, and Californian ambitions literally buried under a thousand basements.

There were two main events in the 1960s that seem to have been critical for the shape of Canadian cities: the completion of the Trans-Canada Highway in 1961 and Centennial Year in 1967. The capturing of the public imagination in Canada around these two events led to all sorts of initiatives too exuberant for ordinary development. The advent of the highway was big in the west; in the older parts of Canada, Ontario, Quebec, and the Maritimes, the Trans-Canada Highway had been cobbled together from existing roadways. The two parts that were new and went where no road had ever gone before were the stretch over Lake Superior between Sudbury and Thunder Bay and the Kicking Horse Pass route through the Rockies. These were heroic projects. In the west, the highway generally follows the CPR main line, as the valleys and passes that were surveyed in 1880s for rail were resurveyed in the 1950s for road. As development had generally followed the rail lines, it was logical that the highway would serve this development. Rail tourism had built Banff and Lake Louise, but road tourism opened the country in a completely different way.

Happy Valley and the idea that one could put in a race track that would rival Mossport was all about harnessing local interests into tourism and revenue generating venues for the good of the city. No idea too grand. Increasingly, it appears that the city administration of Calgary applied the brakes to many proposals that were seen as competing visions of how Calgary should present itself to the world, having been tied for decades to the powerful brand of the old West and the Stampede with all its vested interests. Mossport on the Bow? Didn't fit.

Chapter 28

Sarcee Motor Hotel

The western gate to Calgary, the Paskapoo slopes, a protected reserve, the site of the 1988 Winter Olympics and the 1960s Happy Valley with all its development plans, is an area so complex in its land form and its geographic position in the city that its obvious strategic potential as a gateway seems continually overlooked. Before the opening of the Trans-Canada Highway, the only road going west out of Calgary went to Banff Lake Louise Field and Golden, whereupon one, but only in the summer, could take the Big Bend Highway to Revelstoke. The Trans-Canada changed all that, but not until 1961, which is why this quadrant remained largely undeveloped until the later 1960s, when it became the site of many tourist-related proposals.

One such proposal that was never built was a motor hotel designed by Cohos Evamy Architects for the intersection of Sarcee Trail and Banff Coach Road. It isn't that remarkable as architecture, but it does illustrate some of the thinking about land, tourism, and location in 1970. The motel has restaurant, bar, meeting rooms on the ground floor, and two floors of rooms above. It is a motor hotel, rather than a motel, which tended at the time to be a strip of rooms and a small office. It has, remarkably, parking for 470 cars, indicating much more use was expected than its size suggests. The building footprint is tiny compared to the sea of parking.

Sarcee Trail and Banff Coach Road no longer intersect; with development through the 1970s and 1980s of Prominence Point and Strathcona Park, Bow Trail now links the two roads. Sarcee Trail is an old section road, dead north-south, that once led to Camp Sarcee on the northeast corner of what was known as the Sarcee Reserve, where it ended. It then picked up again south of the reserve as Range Road 21. Going north, the section road reappeared as 55th Street Northwest in Varsity Estates by the University of Calgary and then became

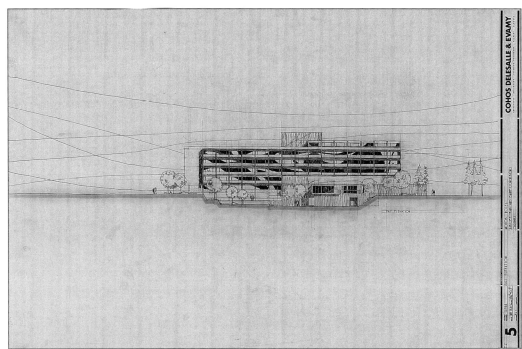

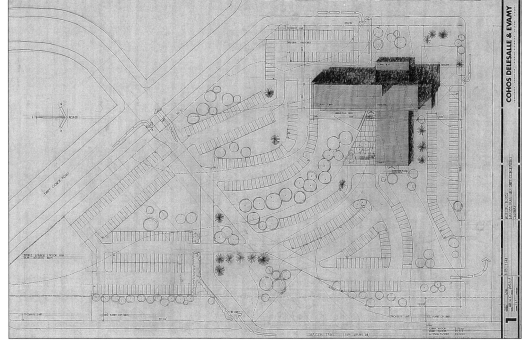

Figure 28-1. This is the east elevation to the project, actually a thin four-storey bar of motel units that float over a concrete base containing the services and public rooms. The reflective nature of the full glass-fronted rooms shows the intention that the motel appears to be a stretched, glittering thing held safely by strong, rough concrete elements. The parking lot, so overwhelming in plan, is just a ground surface. Treed, it would roll away from the building, irrelevant compared to the view looking out over Calgary.
Cohos Evamy fonds. Canadian Architectural Archives, University of Calgary. 57A/79.13, COH 6944.

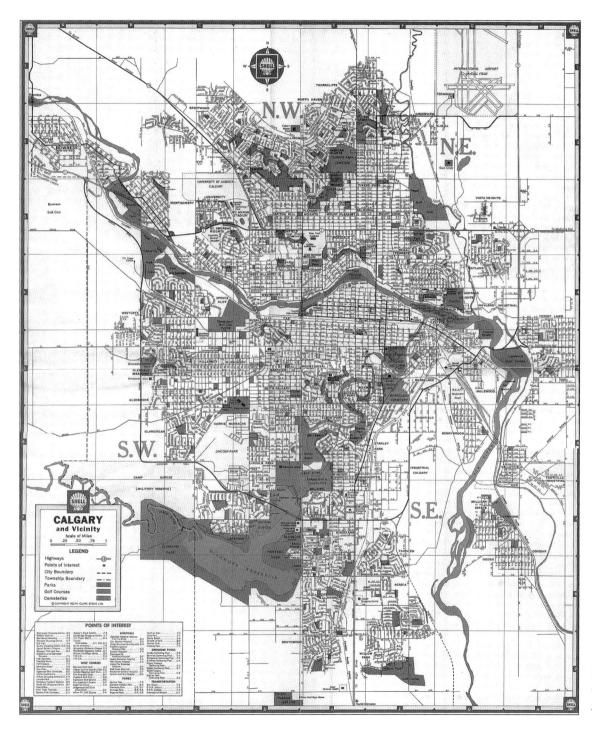

Figure 28.2. Calgary City Map, 1966. *Shell.*

completely lost in the cul-de-sacs of Ranchlands and Hawkwood, where it emerged again to the north as the straight north-south Symons Valley Road, or Highway 772. The Old Banff Coach Road was exactly that: the original road to Banff from Calgary, another section road, Township Road 244. The Trans-Canada Highway appropriated the old Banff Road for much of the Calgary-Banff section.

Until the Trans-Canada rediscovered the Coach Road, the motor route to Banff used what is now known as Highway 1A, which springs from Crowchild Trail within the city limits and passes through Cochrane, the Morley Reserve, Exshaw, and Canmore before arriving at Banff.

This geographical discursion is to show that to locate a hotel at Sarcee and Banff Coach Road anticipated the opening of west Calgary, between the Bow River, the Trans-Canada, and Springbank, a small village directly west of the city. The proposed motor hotel was just too early. Calgary has extensive developments west of Sarcee Trail now, but in 1970 it didn't have any traffic.

HOUSING

Chapter 29

Wheat Boom Subdivisions

The housing landscape of Calgary, because of its boom cycles, falls into distinct and discontinuous eras and styles: inner city, suburban, exurban, and downtown condominium development. These are found in most cities, but in Calgary the balance between the four is not equal, and social mapping of the housing fabric is ambiguous and not always logical. Location and topography often trump convenience.

There is a map from 1907 meant to accompany Henderson's Directories, which were published each year between 1905 and the advent of the internet. The directories covered the Prairie provinces and listed every house and business in the major cities, including a reverse directory so that one can look up a specific address and find who lived in that house, what they did, where they worked, or what the business was at that site. Most libraries hold a set. There are a number of accompanying maps, with various publishers, that constitute a diagram of intention rather than the reality at the time. The Henderson's 1907 map indicates every lot in the city, all the neighbourhood names, even if unbuilt, and a set of radii lines indicating the distance from the centre point of downtown, the CPR station. This is partly a wish list; someone had purchased a piece of land in far off northeast Calgary, divided it up into lots and named it Balaclava Heights; someone else had subdivided their bleak quarter-section homestead in the southwest into streets and avenues and named it after their wife.

The names of these neighbourhoods give a proportional indication of who was in Calgary in the 1900s — and this is just in the northeast sector:

- Pallesen (a Danish surname)
- Manitou Park (Athapascan word for god or spirit)

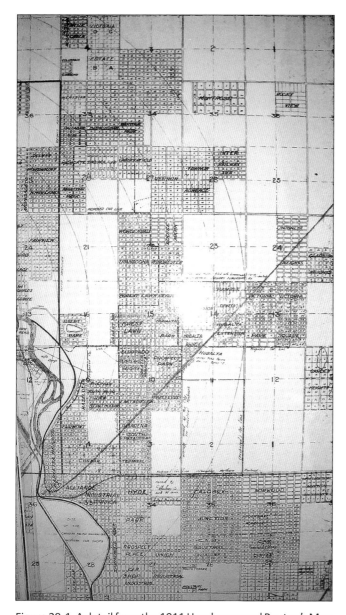

Figure 29-1. A detail from the 1911 Henderson and Ponton's Map (see figure 29-2) showing the east side of Calgary, an area that was developed for housing in the northeast relatively recently (the 1980s to the present) and in the southeast hardly at all.
Courtesy of the Calgary Public Library, Community Heritage and Family History Collection.

- Balfour (prime minister of Great Britain, 1902–1905)
- East Lynne (English 1861 novel by Ellen Wood, a Victorian bestseller about Lady Carlyle, who leaves her husband to elope with an aristocratic cad)
- Claralta (Clara in Alberta)
- Meridian (Calgary is just west of the 5th)
- Birmingham (city in England's West Midlands)
- Highgate (area of north London)
- Balaclava Heights (from the Battle of Balaclava, 1854, and the rout of the Light Brigade)
- Langside (Battle of Langside, 1568, district in Glasgow)
- Northbury (English town)
- Delmar (Spanish for "by the sea" — a southern California seaside resort built in 1885)
- Winona Place (Winona, a small farm town near Niagara Falls)
- Belfast (Northern Ireland)
- Sinclair (Scottish surname)
- Regal Terrace (an aspirational name if there ever was one)
- New Edinburgh (both hopeful and nostalgic)
- St. George's Heights (St .George, patron saint of England)

The population of Calgary in 1884 when the CPR went through was 506. By 1900 it had 4,000 people, a 700 percent increase over 16 years. In 1911 it had 43,704 people, a 992 percent increase in ten years, or a near 100 percent expansion each year. Calgary never expanded this quickly again. Growth was the result of the settlement of the West enabled by the Canadian Pacific Railway, the Grand Trunk Pacific Railway, and Canada's explosive economy at the time. One of the reasons for what is now called the Wheat Boom of the 1900s is the development of dry farming and the 1907 launch of Marquis wheat (a new strain that produced forty-one bushels per acre). The CPR carried grain away to both eastern and western ports for export, and Canada became the largest wheat-exporting country in the world. British mortgage and loan companies saw the Canadian prairies as a secure and stable investment opportunity. In Calgary we can see the accompanying real estate crush in the many subdivisions in the north east. Beginning in 1903 there had been a wheat boom–related jump in immigration and homestead entries for Calgary, sustained until up to the First World War (except for a depression year in 1908). Although the correlation between the wheat boom and Canada's intense period of economic prosperity and expansion has recently been questioned — it wasn't just wheat but also the development of the Canadian steel industry and the rapid expansion of the meat and dairy sector — its effects are evident in the development of all prairie cities, not just Calgary.[1]

Similarly, the 1911 Harrison and Ponton's map (figure 29-2) shows subdivision after subdivision fitting exactly into the quarter sections determined by the 1872 Dominion Land Act as homestead plots, now developed privately, each with their own block and lot size. There was a point where the annual yield of 160 acres planted in wheat was less profitable than selling off forty blocks of forty 25-by-120-foot lots each. To put this in perspective, 1,600 lots per quarter section at $2,000 in 1905 would have returned $3,200,000, or about $300 million today. This was a real estate boom beyond belief. By 1912, that $2,000 lot was $300,000.[2] We know now, after many booms and crashes, how to read the signs, that this is not good.

The property market collapsed in 1913 and thousands of people were left holding property that did not realize its inflated value for another seventy years. Lots were surrendered to the city for defaulted taxes, mortgages walked away from, and men, crushed and broken, lost their minds. The population of Calgary did not decline, but it grew at a more normal rate, 3 percent, until the mid-1950s, when the city grew at 5–6 percent, and the rate has stayed roughly the same since.

---

1   McInnis, *Canadian Economic Development in the Wheat Boom Era*.

2   Prudential Toole Real Estate, "History."

Figure 29-2. Compared to the previous map of 1966 (figure 28-2), one can see how ambitious this map is for 1911. The Dominion Land Survey system provides the underlying land organization. Certain range roads, such as 17th Avenue south, were important in 1911 and are important still.

The site of the university is marked, just west of Roscarrock along the Banff Coach Road, now Bow Trail, with an adjacent subdivision called Varsity Heights. The layout for Shouldice Terrace is on the diagonal of the streetcar line to Bowness, a brave move in an orthogonal grid. Bowness itself is much more relaxed, lining up along the river and much of it clearly still rural. Shouldice Park is marked on the map already, divided into two tree-edged large fields.

There is no military presence here. It took the First World War to put Camp Sarcee on the corner of the Sarcee Reserve, and Lincoln Park was just another proposed quarter-section subdivision. The reservoir just south of Killarney and the open land around it became Currie Barracks in the 1930s, and most of the southern subdivisions were not built until the 1950s.

The Grand Trunk Pacific Railway depot is already on the site of Fort Calgary, and the Stampede racetrack is in place, but at a different angle than it was. Thomas Mawson had not yet laid down his 45 degree axis for the Stampede.

There is a note just above the two sections for Manchester Sub and Industrial Calgary: "Acreage owned by the City in Manchester for Industrial Sites." This became Burnsland, both the cemetery and where all the City of Calgary's infrastructure operations are: the piles of salt and gravel, the hydrants, the trucks, the workshops, and the machinery that run the city.

Map of the City of Calgary, printed for the Hudson's Bay Company. A.P. van Buren, Calgary. Circa 1940.

Wheat Boom Subdivisions [139]

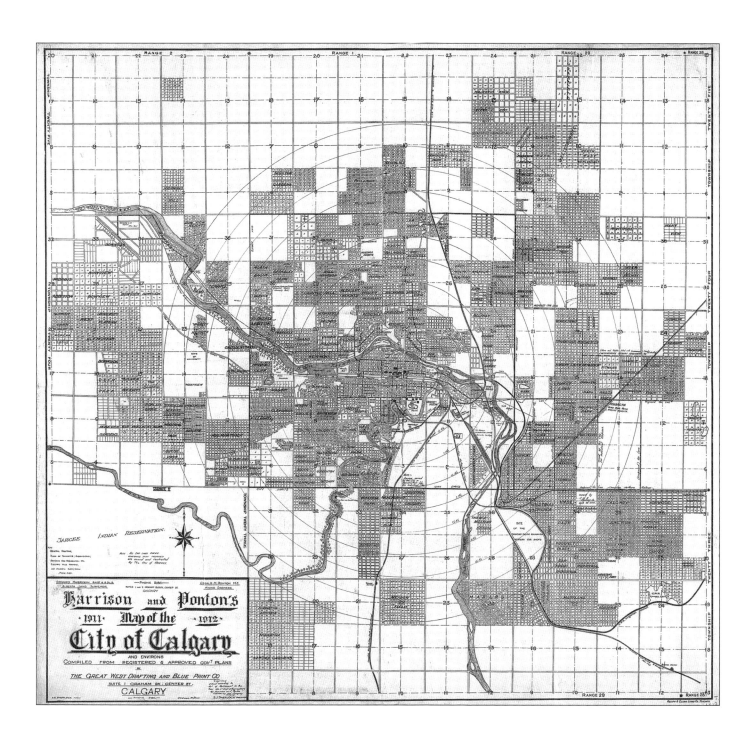

Chapter 30

COMMUNITIES ON LAKES

Not many of these wheat boom subdivisions outside the two mile radius from downtown were built. There is housing there now, but not in their 1907 forms and not called by the same hopeful names. Nonetheless, there were some ideas drawn on the map that were adopted much later in different places. Lakeview Heights clearly needed a lake. If the lake shown on the map in Albert Park is any indication — a low bit of swampy ground that a junior high school and its playing field were built on in the 1950s — Lakeview's body of water was originally also a slough. Interestingly, waterfront lots were not sold, and the lake is democratically ringed by a road.

Sixty years later, in 1967, Lake Bonavista, a Keith Construction development, was built and became the prototype for later lake communities in Calgary. Lake Bonavista and the later Lake Bonaventure were excavated prairie. For Lake Bonavista, some of the 1.2 million cubic yards of excavated dirt were used to build a sixty-five foot hill with a waterfall on it to force water circulation in the lake. The water was originally pumped from Fish Creek, and is now sustained by runoff and an underground spring. There is nothing too democratic about access: both lakes are ringed by houses with private docks, except for the park on Bonavista that contains the hill.

The difference in scale between the 1907 enterprise and the 1967 project is telling, and it possibly has to do with economics. Despite hills being levelled and swales filled (there is a photograph of just this kind of hill removal in Albert Park in 1912), the audacity of man-made lakes is the audacity of wealth. On an earlier model, Chestermere Lake had been made in 1906 by damming Kinniburgh Slough, already a natural depression. The land was part of the original Canadian Pacific Railway land grant and Chestermere was incorporated in the Western Irrigation District as a reservoir for the whole

COMMUNITIES ON LAKES   [141]

Figure 30-1. A promotional postcard for Lakeview Park that hits all the right notes: mountains, a treed promenade around the lake, a pavilion and sailboats, and tidy streets.
Courtesy of the Calgary Public Library, Community Heritage and Family History Collection.

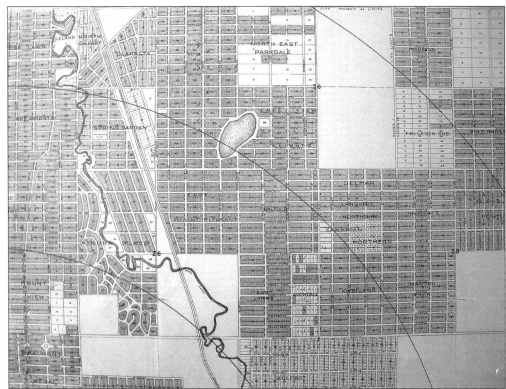

Figure 30-2. Making a virtue of a low marshy piece of land, difficult to build upon.
Courtesy of the Calgary Public Library, Community Heritage and Family History Collection.

system. Cabins were built around the lake on leased lots, but it was not until the mid-70s that the Cabin Owners of Lake Chestermere were able to buy their lots from the Western Irrigation District. Now that Chestermere is a bedroom community for Calgary, its origins as an irrigation reservoir are forgotten.

The more recent manmade lakes within the city of Calgary have no such useful origins, and their role is to increase residential land value, which they do. However, rather than finding natural wetlands and amplifying an already existing environmental condition, these subdivisions appear to be designed on paper, and the land is necessarily re-graded to fit the development diagram. Lake advantage is indisputable; a lake as part of rural prairie landscape is gone.

Chapter 31

Escarpments

Along with swales and hills, rivers and sloughs, another powerful landscape lines both the Elbow and the Bow Rivers and has been colonized for housing with greater and lesser successes. To understand Calgary's escarpments, a little geological background is needed.

When the Laurentide ice sheet, advancing from the northeast, met the Cordilleran ice sheet extending eastwards from the Rocky Mountains, just fifteen thousand years ago, they were covering up a much older topography, the sandstone Paskapoo Formation, about fifty-five million years old. The Bow River had carved the sandstone, made floodplains, and then about twenty-three thousand years ago deposited gravel throughout its valley. This valley was then filled with the two ice sheets, which, when they melted, left behind a layer of till, or what is known as boulder clay. In the process of melting, the Laurentide ice sheet dammed the water melting off the Cordilleran sheet, creating a temporary glacial lake that filled the entire Bow Valley between Nose and Cairn Hills. Fine silt and sand on the lake bed covered the glacial till.

When the water of Lake Calgary finally escaped with the retreat of the Laurentide ice sheet, it cut deep channels through all these accumulated layers, down to the sandstone bedrock. This process ended 13,500 years ago — the glaciers had gone, it was warmer, and the permafrost on the eastern Rocky Mountains began to melt, the Bow River carrying away more glacial till off the mountains and into the valley downstream. This late glacial deposit, the Bighill Creek Formation, finished about twelve thousand years ago, after the glacial sediment from the headwaters of the Bow had mostly been leached away.

Contemporary gravel mining regularly uncovers bones of extinct species, as has foundation excavation on building sites in the downtown area. The animals that lived south of the ice sheets started to migrate north with those sheets' disappearance, including mammoth, camel, caribou, bison, mountain sheep, and two kinds of horse, grazing the grasslands that developed as the Bighill Creek Formation was laid down. The Bow River started to cut its channel through this gravel deposit back down to the sandstone bedrock, and this is the channel it is today. The Bighill Creek gravel included boulders not so easily moved by the river. While it had carried sand and gravel farther downstream, the boulders were left behind, armouring the sides of the Bow River channel at bedrock.

One can see that in the ancient, historic, and contemporary Bow River channel, there were many different glacial, pre-glacial, and post-glacial conditions. It is this that gives the Calgary area its complexity of landforms and determines whether the benches, terraces, and escarpments of both the Bow and Elbow Rivers are stable. A famously entrepreneurial developer, Freddie Lowes of the Canada Life Assurance Company, between 1906 and 1912 — during the real estate boom associated with the wheat boom — built or laid out Elbow Park, Elboya, Windsor Park, and Britannia. From the Oblate Brothers, he bought Mission Hill, annexed by the city in 1907. He had this silty escarpment just downriver from Rideau Park blasted with fire hoses to wash the hill into the Elbow River to form a flat plain, upon which Roxborough was built.[1]

Calgary has always been a city where quite outrageous ideas could be realized. Tom Campbell's Hill, so named because throughout the 1930s there was a huge billboard on it advertising Tom Campbell's Hats, was so unstable that there was an early scheme to permanently freeze it to keep it from sliding down and covering the road at its base. Yet there is a section of adjacent escarpment so stable that east Bridgeland has terraced streets from base to top. Much of this is anecdotal, from memories of Calgarians who were children in its early days: unconfirmable, contrary, but somehow believable.

St. Andrew's Heights

In 1968 a large housing project was proposed for the Bow River escarpment between Toronto Avenue and Sunnyside below, centred on 27th Street Northwest, now in Bowmount Park. Its genesis is interesting; it was a three-day project, a wild proposal by a builder of industrial buildings, mostly in the Highfield area. Karl Pokorny of Saxby & Pokorny Architects did a scheme for 266 units terracing up a fourteen-acre hill. Pokorny, originally from Toronto, had spent a couple of years in London working for the London County Council, one of whose major responsibilities was housing. This was the era of British new towns, council estates, tower block low-income housing replacing old nineteenth-century terraced slums, and rebuilding bombed out sections of the city. Pokorny, as a young architect, had trained in the greatest housing factory of the twentieth century. St Andrew's Heights is a very British plan: it visualises a cohesive, intimate society where shared open space between units expects social propriety and respect. It is the very antithesis of suburban single-family houses, driveways, and fenced-off yards that dominated Calgary then and now.

As a sketch plan, the architecture is not developed, other than its allocation on a steep site. However, the roofs, as seen in the long elevation, are vaulted. This owes something to the developer. All through the Highfield industrial area are workshops with thin shell free-span concrete vaulted roofs. The application of this to a housing project is revolutionary: rather than each house unit being structurally discrete, a bank of house units is treated

---

1   Prudential Toole Real Estate, "History."

Figure 31-1. This map shows an airport site at the top of the escarpment behind Bridgeland. What is unusual is how the cliff was terraced and built upon from bottom to top.
Courtesy of the Calgary Public Library, Community Heritage and Family History Collection.

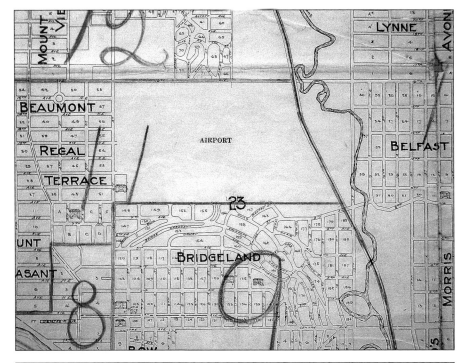

Figure 31-2. In comparison, the cliff under Crescent Heights was not built upon. So it isn't a hard and fast rule that escarpments were unbuildable. Much depends on the particular geology of each portion of escarpment.
Courtesy of the Calgary Public Library, Community Heritage and Family History Collection.

as an industrial workshop under a single roof. There are a number of different strategies: the horizontal banks of units under a single structural unit, single units stepping sideways down the hill, each lower unit acting as a retaining wall for the unit above, and combinations of both.

It is possible that St. Andrew's Heights was one of a series of experimental housing projects proposed in the late 1960s under a Central Mortgage Housing Corporation program looking for innovative housing solutions. However, the site is part of Bowmount Park,

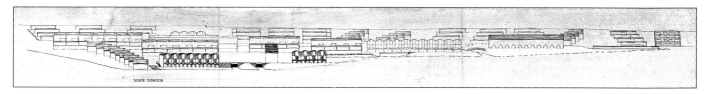

Figure 31-3. Saxby & Pokorny, St. Andrew's Heights, elevation.
Karl Pokorny, Saxby Pokorny Architects, Calgary, Alberta.

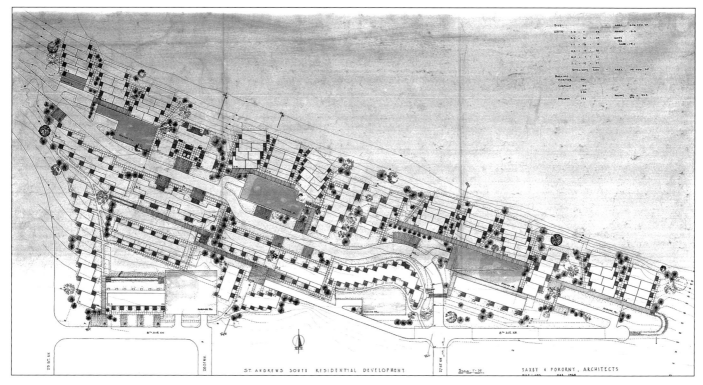

Figure 31-4. Saxby & Pokorny, St. Andrew's Heights, plan.
Karl Pokorny, Saxby Pokorny Architects, Calgary, Alberta.

a long four-kilometre continuous Bow River territory from Montgomery to Silver Springs on the north bank, including Bowness on the south bank. The actual site of St. Andrew's South today is a steep, sandy cliff, easily eroded by dog paths and hiking trails, with exposed clay seams and running springs. A more difficult building site would be hard to find, and as well there was opposition from the surrounding communities. Nevertheless, this project, which had a very short life, introduced a new structural system for housing, a multi-family low-rise complex of co-operative land use unprecedented in the city, on an impossible site. Although it is generally inconceivable today in Calgary that anyone would want to build over the landscape gems that are the escarpments, alongside Edmonton Trail they are being built upon. When one visits Bowmount Park and its grasslands, aspen groves, slices of forest, prairie crocus, asters, orioles, hawks, and kestrels, animals small and large — mule deer, beaver, muskrat, and the ubiquitous coyote — one really does have second thoughts about escarpment development. It is an important part of the Bow River corridor, hopefully to be kept continuous.

This, however, is a twenty-first century view; the 1960s showed a more cavalier attitude to landforms and rivers. Concerns about the environment were just a faint gleam on its horizon. In 1960s Calgary, development gobbled up land in all directions.

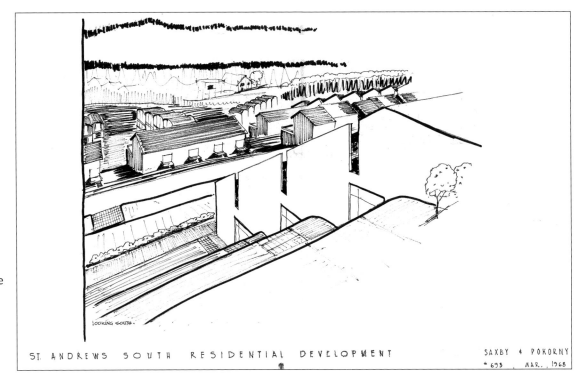

Figure 31-5. At the base of St. Andrew's South escarpment hillside is Hillhurst, small houses, regular streets, beyond is the Bow River and the line of the escarpment on the opposite bank.
Karl Pokorny, Saxby Pokorny Architects, Calgary, Alberta.

REGAL TERRACE

Rick Balbi Architect proposed a large apartment housing unit on an escarpment at the corner of 4th Avenue and Edmonton Trail in 1978, scheduled to begin construction in 1979. Rick Balbi has had a large influence on Calgary through the sheer number of projects his office has been involved with and his long, good working relationship with the City of Calgary. For example, this was a project that was larger than the site was zoned for; however, the planning department and the community both backed it. This particular escarpment hillside was stable and did not present obstacles to construction, although parking was an issue, as digging into the hillside would have required massive retaining walls. Instead, parking was placed above ground, buried in the middle of the project. The building steps down the hill, views are brilliant, so far so good. The owners were developers from Italy who wished to pay the Calgary contractor in units, rather than money, a payment structure that the contractor agreed to. However, the owners then bagged the best units and left less auspicious units for the contractor, who, not surprisingly, was not happy with this and quit the job. By this time, the hot housing market had started to wane and the project was no longer seen as such a desirable commodity — the stoppage on the project propelled the owners in Italy into bankruptcy, and the land was foreclosed by the bank. The land, at this point, could have been snapped up, but Calgary was now in its early 1980s recession and the City of Calgary had changed the zoning to something that would have allowed only half the number of units of the original scheme, making it no longer an attractive economic opportunity.

Development is like a river: you can never step into the same conditions twice. Even six months of global economic changes can make the difference between a project going ahead or not, being a success or not. The land is unchanging, but its potential for development is a constantly shifting surface. .

Figure 31-6. East elevation.
Rick Balbi Architect, Calgary, Alberta.

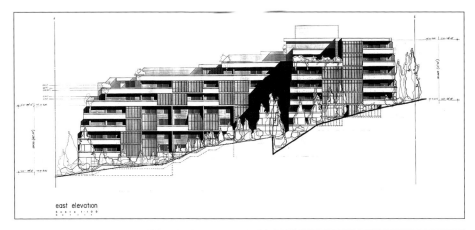

Figure 31-7. The north elevation, where it faces a regular neighbourhood, is just a handsome late 1970s apartment building with glassed-in and open balconies, not too regular, not too haphazard, no indication of the rest of the project tumbling down the hill behind it.
Rick Balbi Architect, Calgary, Alberta.

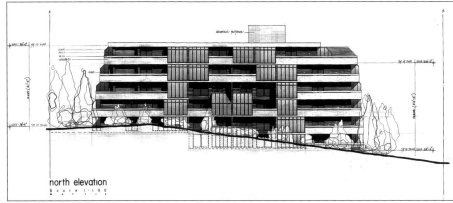

Figure 31-8. There is a great confidence shown in this very large project on a challenging site. While the 1968 proposal for St. Andrew's South spreads a community over a wide hillside, this project builds that community into something as solid as a new landform. The indication of balconies full of plants is more than just decoration for the drawing — it implies that the building is a hillside itself, with its own surface.
Rick Balbi Architect, Calgary, Alberta.

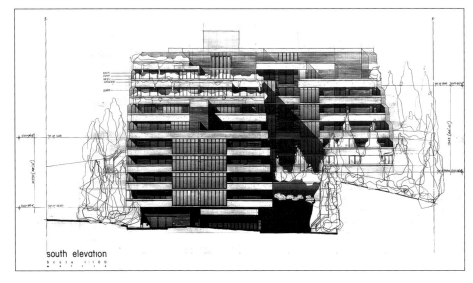

Chapter 32

Hills

It is one thing to build on the side of a hill, another to build on top of it. In Calgary there are two such landscapes: either the plateau at the top of the escarpments, or on the top of hills in the foothill formations themselves.

Two projects, separated by several decades, look at the possibilities of elevation.

Earth-Sheltered Housing

This was a house for a zoology professor at the University of Alberta at Calgary, in 1962. Gordon Atkins's comments about this project are, as usual, pithy:

> Being one of the highest hills in the nearby area, the site is extremely bare, cold and exposed. From the hill there is a distant view of the city, the mountains and the Bow Valley (approximately 180°) The client was an 'easterner' and therefore revelled in the unhampered glory of exposure. To offset this un-Canadian desire, the building was submerged, partially, and backed into the hill.
>
> The client was initially receptive and had a direct architectural awareness that sets him apart from most clients. This awareness can however become as negative as ignorance. Finally as a result of indecision and demands made by the client which were not within the scope of an economical solution the project was abandoned.
>
> Construction: poured in place concrete, prairie sod roof, warm air heated from hollow floor slab, $25,000 cost estimate.[1]

---

1 P.K. Anderson Residence drawing.

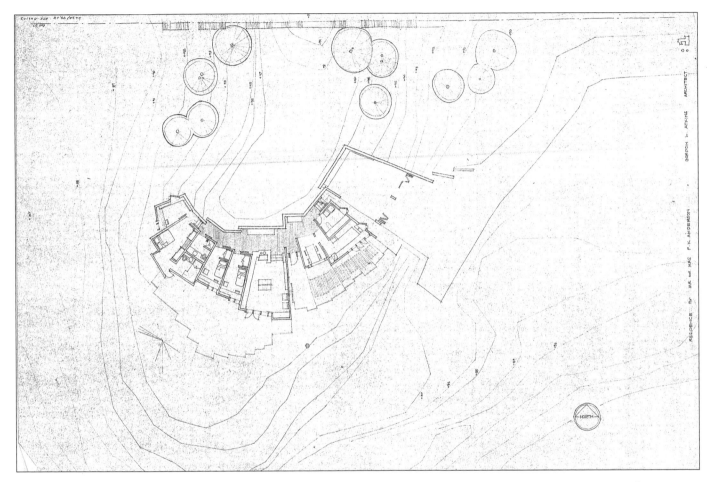

Figure 32-1. There is almost nothing to date this house. It could be done today. The garage door does not shout down the driveway; it is shielded by a series of retaining walls. The kitchen is very generous and opens onto a wide terrace and the dining room is too small for contemporary furniture, which has caught the gigantic disease, but no matter — spare 1950s Danish modern has a rediscovered cachet. All the rooms fan out so that the view side is the widest wall. The back wall is minimized, as is the main circulation for the house, an arc of a back hallway, skylit, in some places as wide as a living room itself. The bedrooms seem a bit small for today, but one would rather have one of these rooms than a plain box twice the size. Each room has a slightly different view — from kitchen to the little end study is a 90 degree difference in angle.

Gordon Atkins fonds. Canadian Architectural Archives, University of Calgary. 263A/99.02, ATK A62.03.

Oh, those clients. A little awareness is a dangerous thing. Before he came to Calgary, Professor Anderson lived in Berkeley; San Francisco glories in its hills. Other than Atkins's post-project pissed-offness, we can only surmise the problems this house ran into. What is interesting about it is how early this earth-sheltered, sod-roofed, heated-floor slab, fan-shaped house was. Earth sheltering only began to appear in environmentally conscious house-building books in the mid-1970s, after the 1973 OPEC crisis and as part of a counter-cultural movement to recover ancient forms of building.

Frank Lloyd Wright used radiant heat floors in his Usonian houses of the late 1930s, and in the 1950s, Joseph Eichler in California built housing on a large scale with

Figure 32-2. This somewhat disappointing drawing indicates a series of conventional windows and the drawing itself lacks love. One wonders if this is when disenchantment between client and architect had set in.
Gordon Atkins fonds. Canadian Architectural Archives, University of Calgary. 263A/99.02, ATK A62.03.

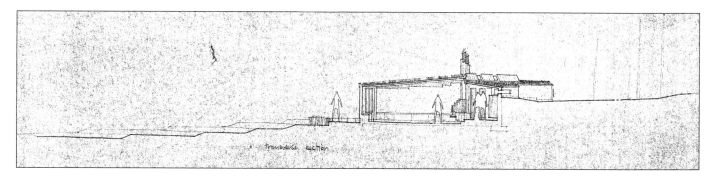

Figure 32-3. From this section, through the living room it looks like, the back hall seems a very interesting place, skylit, with a sloping ceiling and an odd, rambling shape. The rooms with their south-facing windows would have felt dramatically different: open, full of light, and taller.
Gordon Atkins fonds. Canadian Architectural Archives, University of Calgary. 263A/99.02, ATK A62.03.

in-floor heating. A National Research Council bulletin of 1963 outlines the research on polyethylene pipe laid in concrete slabs[2] — poly pipe was just ten years old and the research came from Germany and Britain. Although apartments, offices, and stores used radiators, natural gas hot air was how city houses traditionally were heated. In 1962, in Calgary, the radiant floor was a pretty obscure form of residential heating. And when something is obscure, it becomes expensive.

Poured-in-place concrete was also an unusual construction method for a house. The 1922 Schindler House in Los Angeles would have been, for a young architect in 1962, the iconic modern example of a concrete house. For Atkins, building a house set into a hillside would automatically use retaining walls needed to hold back the weight of the slope. A concrete roof slab to hold a turfed roof, plus the foundation-floor slab, would indicate an economy of means if concrete was used for everything. This, however, was Calgary. Postwar subdivisions had spread over the prairies like grass fire, and these were mostly inexpensive wood-frame single-storey bungalows or split-level ranch houses on flat lots. Atkins's innovative, sensible, and unusual house would have had difficulty in finding an equally adventurous contractor. The average house price in 1962 was $12,500, just half the estimated cost of construction for this house. Any contractor would have covered his back by inflating his price when dealing with such an eccentric project.

It is interesting to compare this project with the Saxby & Pokorny 1967 proposal for South St. Andrews — again, this was housing built as a series of concrete retaining walls and slabs on a hillside, both projects using construction methods borrowed from light industrial construction.

---

2 Platts, R.E, *Where Polyethylene Pipe Challenges Metal for Slab Radiant Heating.*

Such a project wouldn't have been such a stretch for an industrial builder as it was for Atkins's contractor, who most likely built more conventional flat-land houses.

Four Square House and Subdivision

In 1996 south Canyon Meadows was typical of an edge-of-the-city parcel of land, recently used for agriculture then zoned as acreages, then allowed to be developed into higher density housing. The neighbourhood is bounded by Anderson Road, MacLeod Trail, and Fish Creek Park. It contains a golf course, an LRT station, a shopping centre, and about eight thousand people. This project was for a parcel on the north side of Fish Creek Valley, overlooking Fish Creek Park; the client did not want a suburban housing project typical of new communities in Calgary.

The suburban housing model typically flattens the land into easily buildable sites. Despite topographic difference being desirable today in many neighbourhoods — Mount Royal, Ramsay and Bankview come to mind — it has not always been so in the past, and is not so for blanket housing developments. Prairie or rangeland is usually re-graded to make the installation of services easier, to make roads safer in the winter, and to transform something that might be objectionably rural into something aspirationally suburban. The site for this particular project is at the top of an escarpment with a long view across Fish Creek Valley. The top of escarpments tend to be flat already, and this site has the advantage of a view. The task of the architect, Gerald Forseth, was to give each house a view of the natural landscape rather than the view of the house across the street and over the back fence. Another task was to avoid the wide blank facades that dominate so much suburban housing, the client sharing this dislike with many of the New Urbanism neighbourhoods such as if significant land forms become privately owned, the view of them is a public commodity. It is a case of aspect and prospect, what a building looks like and what it looks upon, and the corollary, who sees the building and where are they when they see it. The view from Calgary's public landscapes is often of the very best houses along the most expensive streets. Surprisingly, this lack of privacy, the very opposite of the premise of gated communities, imposes a rough and healthy democracy on Calgary's residential districts.

GEOLOGY AND METAPHOR

Chapter 33

Geology and Geography

Why is it so important to keep in touch with Calgary's original geography, no matter how overlaid it becomes by development and urban programming? The land, the climate, the weather, our geology, gives us our perspective. The horizon is where we, as urbanites, see where in the world we are.

Calgary has two important horizons. Nose Hill is protected; where the grass meets the sky is scaleless. It seems far away and gives us a kind of distance in our view of the surroundings. The Tsuu T'ina Nation is another such horizon, and it dominates the long view to the southwest of the city. In contrast, Edgemont is a subdivision built around the bottom of a ridge in northwest Calgary. Topping the ridge is a clutch of houses with a marvellous view, no doubt, creating a wonderful prospect, but the aspect, what it looks like to the rest of us, is to limit our vision. The top of the hill, instead of looking distant as does Nose Hill, looms directly overhead. Seeing details on houses makes them seem extremely close and the scale becomes overly taut.

This is all about optical illusion, not a trick, but an understanding of how a city makes deep visual connections to its environment and to its hinterland. On the rare days that one cannot see the mountains, Calgary feels as if it is a lonely spaceship, floating without horizon. Being able to see the mountains is an important part of this city's identity, its context; it is tied to the greater geomorphology of the Rocky Mountains to the west, and to the east, the ancient Bassano Basin, the two views from any downtown high-rise tower.

From the ground, in the downtown area, there are still views of the bleached grass on the escarpments above the Bow River. No matter how windy and gritty and grey is the downtown, there is this visual reminder that there is a steep slope winding along by the river. It reminds us that there is a river. This is important. It keeps our attention from becoming too inward; it gives us a context for the intensity of the downtown core. It is a relief valve. And yet, so much of it is still vulnerable to development — Edmonton Trail cuts straight up an escarpment. Development on the west side of Edmonton Trail is almost complete, and steep streets and stacked apartments lean back on the hillside. On the east side of Edmonton Trail, development is slow but continuous. The escarpment in this area is merely considered to be a difficult building site rather than anything more meaningful.

The relationship between aspect and prospect underpinned the English landscape tradition of the eighteenth century and still underpins much of our contemporary sense of the picturesque: they must be in balance. It is not just a condition one might apply to individual buildings. Aspect is what we see when we look *at* a city. Too much attention to aspect, to the dazzling nighttime view, for example, which has become one of Calgary's iconic images, means that urban decisions are made according to appearance and status. Too much prospect, what one sees *from* one's vantage point in a building or in a city, leads to an unseemly jostling for view, for position, for the treasured view of the mountains, or for the very few lots that front on a river.

Ironically, much of twentieth-century development did not value the Bow River. There was no jostling for a riverside property — it was dangerous. The escarpments were often unstable and so were not valued much either. For the top of the Ramsay escarpment that overlooks the Stampede grounds, Scotchman's Hill (the cheap seats, think blankets and picnics on the grass, watching the races), its prospect was everything, and its aspect was irrelevant. When houses are built along the tops of escarpments, their aspect is made both visible and diminished.

Does it matter that we know that for every river there is a cliff, cut ten thousand years ago? Probably not. We have more important things occupying our attention. However, nature gives calm. It presents itself as noble and eternal, things that calm us by merely being next to it. To lose this from a city is a tragedy. What we find with the Calgary Tower of 1966, or the PetroCan Building of 1978, or the Bow Building of 2012, is that specimen buildings, usually notable for their height, become the aspect; they are the iconic skyline of Calgary, more remarkable than Calgary's prospect of the mountains and its grain-growing and ranching hinterland landscapes, of which the escarpments, threaded into the civic park system, are the last vestiges.

Penny Lane Towers

Two projects may be discussed here in terms of capturing the particular environmental qualities of Calgary. They are separated by thirty years, but are united by a commitment to a geological and climactic reality. Barry Johns's 1988 Winter Olympics Arch was discussed earlier, in part 26, as an encapsulation of Calgary's environment of mountains, the wind that blows off them, and the Chinook Arch.

The sensibility found in Johns's Olympic Arch of 1988 carries through to another Calgary project, the development of the Penny Lane site, 8th to 9th Avenues between 4th and 5th Streets Southwest. This project by Gibbs Gage Architects was programmed originally for two office towers, one thirty-storeys and the other forty-five. Barry Johns was a joint venture partner in the design and presented a series of geological and environmental metaphors for what is often seen as an intractable building type: the office tower with +15 and +30 connections and an obligatory plaza. Johns proposed a "cascading ice

GEOLOGY AND GEOGRAPHY   [161]

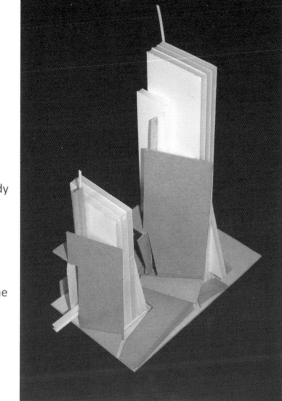
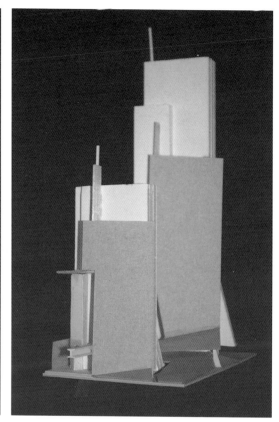

Figure 33-1. There is always something so engaging about little study models of foam core and bits of cardboard: it is architectural form at its most direct, before materials, before structural systems. One has the program and the world this program is going to occupy. The architecture is how it does this.
Barry Johns Architects Ltd., Edmonton, Alberta.

Figure 33-2. In this, the earliest proposal for Penny Lane Towers, the main office towers are thin slabs facing east-west, with more complex and deeper space in the lower halves. Compared to the existing buildings around the site, this project attempted a complexity of form to support a metaphor, over a more pragmatic envelope.
Barry Johns Architects Ltd., Edmonton, Alberta.

wall that falls off the façade to an angled cascade at the ground plane, facing the south west mountains, setting up the basic parti for a base, a podium and twin towers that defer to this one big gesture" — that gesture derived from winter, the geological collision that produced the Rocky Mountains, and the dramatic replication of sliding and uplifting plates of ice that occurs every winter on the Bow River.

The project, of which the original study models are shown here, was awarded a development permit in 2002, but there was a slight downturn in the market at the time. When it picked up again, a few years later, new partners constituted the development group, which, still retaining Gibbs Gage Architects, simplified the towers somewhat to those we see on the site today as Eight Avenue Place. Their current elegant and restrained shapeliness has liquefied the ice sheets of the original proposal. This is a case where the details were unbuilt, but the intentions were so strong as to pull through all the complexity of the design and construction process.

NEIGHBOURHOODS

Chapter 34

Calgary's Quadrants

It is perhaps worth looking at the overall shape of residential Calgary here to give some sort of context to the different projects in this book. Calgary didn't develop evenly out from the central core. Why is there so much housing in the southwest and the north? Why is there so much industry in the southeast? If we look at how Calgary organized itself into neighbourhoods, communities, and districts, there are, from the beginning, developers with individual visions for subdivisions. Even during the hectic real estate market of the late wheat boom, when quarter sections were divided up into house plots, there was still attention given to character, usually embodied in the name. After the Second World War, in a second building boom associated with postwar possibilities and optimism, we find a new wave of subdivisions being carved out on quarter sections of farmland. These are late 1950s neighbourhoods of churches and parks, wide lots and trees, apartments and schools, and similar later developments extend south along Elbow Drive for several miles. Photographs of these districts in construction show they were laid out on land as flat and featureless as a board, sandwiched between north-south traffic arteries of MacLeod Trail, Elbow Drive, 14th Street, and Crowchild Trail.

The northeast quadrant follows much the same pattern despite being southwest Calgary's economic opposite: neighbourhoods are laid out between Deerfoot Trail and its associated industrial corridor, Blackfoot Trail, 35th Street and 52nd Street. The north-south series of neighbourhoods that were built between 35th and 52nd Streets extend north to the airport, which they skirt to the east and then continue on.

In the southwest there are several immovable natural formations within the city limits, particularly the Bow and Elbow River Valleys, which cut deeply into the sandy soil to create sharp escarpments and flood plains. The Elbow River, which comes directly off the Kananaskis Range just

120 kilometres away, has very steep sides and little flat land not susceptible to June floods. Its neighbourhoods become exclusive because of their containment. That these neighbourhoods do flood still shows the perilous nature of building on such sandy soil so close to the mountains.

In 1932 the Elbow River was dammed at Weaslehead and the Glenmore Reservoir was created as both a water supply and for flood control. The reservoir ate up a piece of the Sarcee Reserve, isolating the northeast corner of the most eastern township of the three townships allocated to the Sarcee, now the Tsuu T'ina. This isolated corner had been appropriated during the First World War by the Department of National Defence for Camp Sarcee, and it stayed as a Canadian Forces Base until 1996. Camp Sarcee was a military training site full of strategic positions, overlooks, rivers to ford, coulees, and generally rugged terrain, in use up until land claims processes started to retrieve lost reserve land all across Canada. Historically, the Glenmore Reservoir, the Sarcee Reserve, the Elbow River, and the military landscape of southwest Calgary presented a non-negotiable zone in the city to which all development has deferred.

In the southeast, a different kind of non-negotiable territory — different from landforms and reservoirs — dominates the sector. Patrick Burns was a vastly wealthy, philanthropic landholder who had made a fortune supplying provisions for the construction of the Grand Trunk Pacific Railway, later the Canadian National Railway. In the early 1900s, the Burns Ranch of twenty-thousand acres extended from what is now Stampede Park to 146 Avenue South, from MacLeod Trail to the Bow River, in other words, the entire south east quadrant of the city. His other holdings stretched in a continuous territory from Cochrane to the U.S. border, a distance of 250 kilometres, and included many other ranches between Calgary and Red Deer. One can be staggered by the numbers in Burns's story — his land assets alone were 2,800 square kilometres (700,000 acres), but more to the point of this book is his influence on the development of Calgary. His ranching empire extended right into the southeast corner of the downtown core with the Burns Building at 9th Avenue and 2nd Street East. This was a cream-coloured seven-storey terracotta office building, the ground floor of which was a meat market. This building was a block away from the CPR main line, and just across the Elbow River, and also on the CPR line was his stockyard, abattoir, and meat packing plant. These sites are now considered inner-city sites, a short walk from the downtown core. The stockyards stopped operating as such in 1975 and the land is now re-developed as an inner city industrial park, while the meat packing plant was decommissioned shortly after and is now a market; all that remains of this particular meat processing landscape is the St. Patrick Hotel, the local watering hole for the Stampede, the stockyard and the meat packing plant.

MacLeod Trail divides east from west in south Calgary, and, roughly parallel, the Bow River winds its way through the middle of the southeast quadrant, flanked by light and sometimes heavy industry and manufacturing until it pulls free of the twentieth century into a wide zone of new communities on Calgary's southeast edge. One can tell from the name of several industries, such as Burnco, the concrete and gravel company, that they are part of the Burns holdings. In Burnco's case, the millions of years it took for the Bow River to cut its way through the loess and till left by the melting Laurentide ice sheet resulted in great deposits of gravel throughout the city. In the unpaved back alleys of today's Calgary, the river run gravel is a tangible sign of both deep geologic history and the of the Burns industry that mined it.

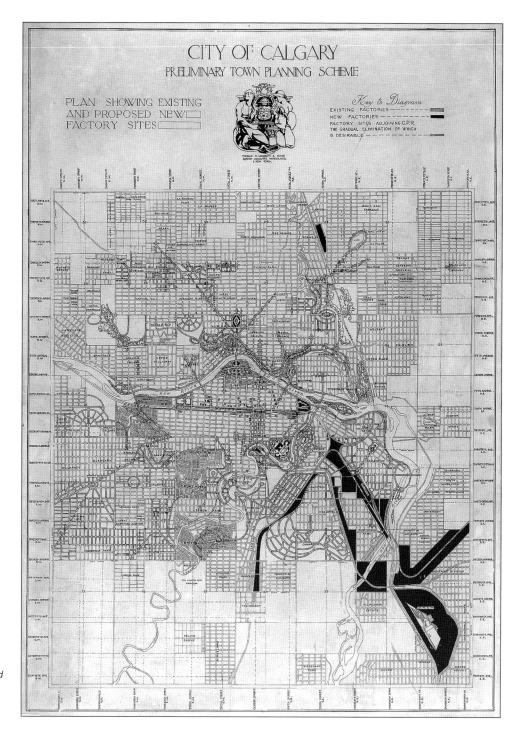

Figure 34-1. How Mawson worked can be seen in this plan. It is clearly based on the commercial plans, such as figure 29-1, into which he has drawn interventions: axies, crescents, and circuses. He introduces diagonals to the relentless Dominion Land Survey grid. In the key to the diagram are existing factories (hatched), new factories (black), and "factory sites adjoining CPR, the gradual elimination of which is desirable" (grey). Again, we find the divide between the City of Calgary and the CPR. Mawson was not the CPR's friend. Nevertheless, those great black swathes through the southeast quadrant were CPR, Grand Trunk Pacific, and Pat Burns land. This was less a proposal and more a confirmation of reality.
Thomas Mawson, Plan Showing Existing and Proposed New Factory Sites. City of Calgary Preliminary Town Planning Scheme, 1911.

[168] Unbuilt Calgary

Figure 34-2. This is a detail from the Burton aerial drawing of 1910, showing the complexity of railway activities in the southeast. The racetrack at the Calgary Stampede serves to orient us. St George's Island and the present-day zoo is the large island in the Bow River at the top of the image. Ramsay is the hill to the east of the Elbow River.

H.M. Burton, "Bird's Eye View of Calgary, 1910." Calgary Engraving Company.

There is some housing throughout the southeast quadrant, the neighbourhoods south of 17th Avenue Southeast, perched high above the river, such as the 1981 Erin Woods, Millican Estates, or Lynnview Ridge, also built in the early 1980s housing boom, on the site of an old oil refinery. It was found to be so contaminated that there was a decade long legal battle to either compensate homeowners or to have the land decontaminated, which it was by 2009. The inner southeast quarter has always been, since the beginning of Calgary, an industrial zone. And towns such as Ogden, or Ceepeear, settlements originally attached to CPR yards, are small islands in an industrial sea.

If one was from Mars, or one of the thousands of people from somewhere else in Canada considering a move to Calgary and looking at a map, Ogden, Millican, Lynnwood, and Valleyfield would appear to be very desirable. On the Bow River which is now lined with bike paths and riverine parks, they contain intimate streets, old housing fabric, and, if one spoke to anyone in Ogden, tremendous community spirit. However, these were wheat, rail, and real estate boom neighbourhoods, thrown up quickly and arehumble, even today without cachet. It is one of Calgary's ironies that the beautiful Bow River is still lined with unprosperous and environmentally compromised neighbourhoods dating from either the 1910–1912 real estate boom or the 1978–82 second oil boom.

Chapter 35

Mawson/Manchester

One of the generally overlooked plans in the Mawson proposal to remake Calgary is an artisan's neighbourhood in Manchester, currently a light industrial area east of MacLeod Trail, between Burnsland Cemetery and 50th Avenue. Manchester was designated in 1914 as a small neighbourhood along 2nd Street supporting what was then known as the Central Industrial Area, made up of workshops and light industrial buildings flanking a Canadian Pacific Railway line that ran south to Fort MacLeod, parallel to MacLeod Trail.

Mawson, 1912

Mawson's proposal is seen in *Detail Plan Describing Arrangement of Workmens Area, Manchester District*. What we have is the CPR tracks at the top of the drawing, faced with factory sites. These brownfield sites are screened by a hedged boulevard from a Beaux-Arts, formal, axial arrangement of about thirty-two variously sized blocks of small semi-detached houses drawn out as "English Artisans Detached and Semi-Detached Dwellings," essentially arts and crafts cottages, "for adaptation." A recreation ground with an oval running track around a playing field completes the formal set piece.

To arrange working-class life as the domestic sandwiched between the factory and the sports ground borrows much from the Workers' Sports Movement of the late nineteenth and early twentieth centuries, part of the then-new concept of leisure, a by-product of industrialization. Sport was the preserve of the privileged until the rise of labour politics founded in middle-class socialism promoted the export of workers' sport throughout the "international proletariat."[1] The utopian ideals of the Arts and Crafts movement, based on the writings of John Ruskin and led by the socialist William Morris, while not

---

1 Wheeler, "Organized Sport and Organized Labour."

able to banish industrial life, did aim to enrich workers' lives. They were not to be cogs in the factory process, but human beings with a social, intellectual, and healthy environment in which to grow. The smokey back-to-back terraces of nineteenth-century British mill towns were meant to be replaced by, eventually, the garden city. This clearly utopian element in Mawson's proposals was also lodged in a romantic nationalism, the export of the Anglo-Saxon destiny of the British Empire, of which Canada was a part.

Fundamentally, Mawson was a garden designer for large houses and public parks. He lectured in garden design at Liverpool University and in 1923 became the president of the Town Planning Institute of Great Britain; planning and garden design were clearly closely allied at the beginning of the twentieth century. In 1911 he published *Civic Art*, his principles of town planning. This is precisely the year that he began the elaborate plan for Calgary.

In a review of Janet Waymark's *Thomas Mawson: Life, Gardens and Landscapes*, Walter Cook describes how the late Victorian class system accorded gardeners a fairly low position. Mawson's ambition was to be more than a gardener and more than a self-described landscape architect who had risen through the trade without architectural training. He wanted to be a town planner. It is important to remember this when considering his plan for Calgary, which can be seen as a detailed illustration of his 1911 manifesto, *Civic Art*.

The Arts and Crafts movement, which had so influenced Mawson, was predicated on recovering a pre-industrial English past and led to hugely influential concepts such as the Garden Suburb, the Garden City, and in the United States, the City Beautiful. In reaction to the outmoded English picturesque, aristocratic landscape tradition of the early 1800s, by the end of the nineteenth century a series of revival movements drove both architecture and gardens into an increasingly formal, Italianate, hedged and parterred garden style. Mawson's plan for Manchester is essentially a formal garden in which factory workers would live. A similar Garden City neighbourhood was built in Halifax after the 1917 Halifax explosion that demolished the northern

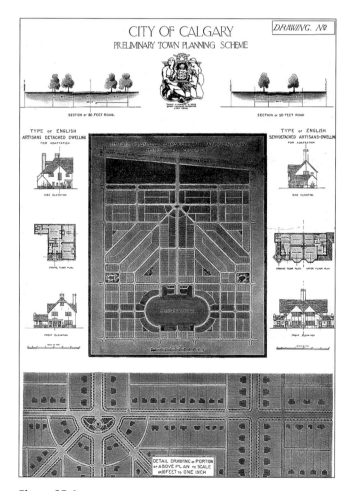

Figure 35-1.

Thomas Mawson, City of Calgary Preliminary Town Planning Scheme, 1911.

slopes of the city. The Hydrostone, as it is called, consists of 324 houses on wide boulevards for the working class Haligonians made homeless by the explosion. At the time it was criticized as being too elegant for workers; a similar critique would have been levelled at a rebuilt Manchester. The Hydrostone today is a very desirable place in which to live — a classic garden suburb set piece. Had Mawson's Manchester been built, it would have changed the nature of the immediate southeast quadrant. Such a project, built for workers, but better than the neighbourhoods being thrown together for the middle classes, would have immediately gentrified, and the 1960s strip development along MacLeod Trail would have been forced to start farther south. This neighbourhood would have given more *gravitas* to the poplar avenue that Patrick Burns planted, on MacLeod Trail at Cemetery Hill as the south gateway to the city. The poplar avenue would have been maintained, balancing Centre Street Bridge, the northern gateway to the city.

As it was, the property development market crashed and a few houses were eventually built along 2nd Street. A 1924 aerial photograph does not show any building in the area; however, with development along MacLeod Trail, by the 1950s enough housing had accumulated to have an elementary school, and Manchester peaked in 1968 with eight hundred residents. It then began a slow decline into auto body shops, warehouses, and strips of automotive repair industries.

The Manchester Area Redevelopment Plan

The Manchester Area Redevelopment Plan, proposed in 2003 and adopted in 2008, presents new images of a future Manchester, no less utopian than Mawson's, but with more likelihood of coming true. Its goals are to "establish a vital residential community with local commercial uses that are compatible with the existing adjacent general light industrial uses … providing accommodation close to employment opportunities, and protecting existing industrial uses from residential encroachment."[2] This means a spine of small-scale live/work units in existing houses and new medium to high density residential units separated from the CPR and the LRT tracks by a broad band of industrial development and from MacLeod Trail by a thinner band of general commercial development. A park is pressed between the high-rise residential and the industrial zone. Suggestions for the enhanced pedestrian area show a leafy village street of sidewalk cafés and strolling couples.

To quote from the redevelopment plan document, "the design of buildings, park spaces, pathways and parking areas should adhere to the principles of Crime Prevention Through Environmental Design: encourage 'eyes on the street' through the placement of windows, porches and balconies."[3] The document carries on in this vein, outlining the nature of a future Manchester. There will be a community garden occupying part of the park. The ARP has a time frame of ten to fifteen years and provides a guideline for the City of Calgary when new development proposals for the area come their way. There are new projects in Manchester, and a low-income apartment was built on the site of the old school and several more are in construction. The school grounds are now a park, and a row of medium density townhouses and apartments faces it on the west side while

---

2 Manchester Area Redevelopment Plan, The City of Calgary Planning and Transportation Policy document, 2008.

3 Manchester Area Redevelopment Plan, The City of Calgary Planning and Transportation Policy document, 2008.

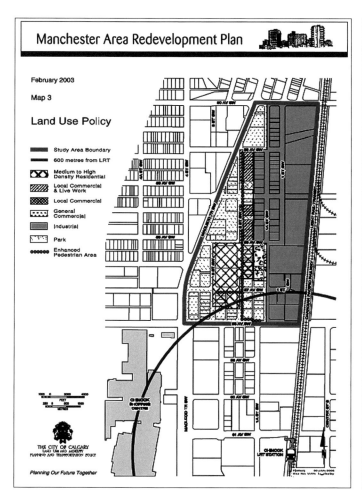 

Figure 35-2. Manchester Area Redevelopment Plan, February 2003. This is a surprising area in redevelopment. It isn't completely built, and therefore there is the potential, depending on future economic climate change, for the entire area to be partially unbuilt. However, for now, it is turning out to be a quiet, well-proportioned, medium- to high-density district. The power of these drawings, which represent development ideologies, is that, like Mawson's drawings (see figure 35-1), they can always be revisited, picked up again, even decades later, and parts found that will still suit.
City of Calgary Planning Department Manchester Area Redevelopment Plan.

a retail and office strip faces it on the east side. One can see the intentions. The Manchester ARP takes the long view and must wait for the increasing pressure for inner-city housing (rather than development at the edges of the city) to begin to override the property economics of light industrial land use.

This 2003–08 vision for Manchester is based on the liveable city, of which Greenwich Village was the original exemplar, followed by many of the neighbourhoods in Toronto. It is a powerful image, the village in the city, and persists for good, humanist reasons. Mawson's plans were based on the idea that the city was a garden, Edenic and egalitarian. Neither premise has taken Calgary as it was and as it is seriously. This is a city of rapacious growth interspersed with doldrums of despair, a rich city with little class solidarity; rather, there is eternal aspiration. Nevertheless, and this repeats itself throughout Calgary's developmental history, none of this is any reason not to propose achievable schemes represented by very seductive images. Manchester could become a self-sustaining live/work neighbourhood, as the infrastructure and some of the ARP proposals are already in place. However, Calgary's transportation networks privilege extremely efficient car travel, its public transportation less so, and jobs and careers change with such frequency that to purchase a house close to work would be a nearly irrelevant factor. Mawson proposed a utopian workers' state, the ARP proposes a utopian village. They will come to pass, both of them, just in an extremely long time frame.

Chapter 36

Inner-City Neighbourhood Main Streets

There are a series of small main streets in the inner city: 9th Avenue Southeast in Inglewood, 10th Street in Sunnyside, 4th Street in Mission, lower Edmonton Trail in Bridgeland, and 11th Street Southwest in lower Mount Royal. They date from the era of streetcars and local shops and services: 1900s brick buildings, one to two storeys, interspersed with equally ordinary and humble buildings that filled in between them over the next fifty years. When the 1950s and early 60s building and oil boom occurred and subdivisions leapt out of the inner city river valley communities to the plateaus of the escarpments above, these inner-city neighbourhoods became progressively more shabby, less economically advantaged, and full of aging populations and small houses. In the United States, such neighbourhoods became the home of African-Americans and Latino immigrants, precipitating the white flight from the downtown and inner-city cores of most American cities in favour of the suburbs. In Canada the divide wasn't racial — it tended to be economic.

Inglewood, for example, was a working-class Canadian Pacific Railway neighbourhood squeezed between the CPR main line, the Elbow River, a Canadian National Railway line, the Bow River, and Alyth Yards, the big marshalling and repair CPR shops. Another example, Riverside, now incorporated into Bridgeland, dates from the early 1890s as a German settlement, when most men were working for either the CPR, the Calgary Brewery, or, by 1911, the Riverside Lumber Company, and the area was only annexed by the city in 1910. Bridgeland itself was an Italian settlement, dominated by the General Hospital, a major employer throughout the area. Inglewood was cursed with the stigma of being east of the downtown core — because North America's prevailing winds blow from the west, downwind east sides of cities usually are the sites of industry and have less clean air. Inglewood and 9th Avenue, its three-block main street, were considered rough, insalubrious, and of no real estate value despite being on the Bow River and just a twenty-minute walk to the Hudson's Bay store, long considered the public heart of downtown. Thus, it was completely ignored as a site of potential development and revitalization until the middle of the 1990s, when planning theory caught up with its charm, its human scale, and its location. The working-class origins of many of these small immigrant settlements contributed to a slowing down of development potential, preserving them well into the 1980s, even the 2000s, with their scale and buildings intact.

Hillhurst-Sunnyside, north of the Bow River, was rediscovered a bit earlier, in the late 1970s with the second oil boom. This area, within a brisk walk of the centre of downtown, did not have the stigma of being in the east end; it was between the Bow River and the Southern Alberta Institute of Technology on the hill above it. It contains the elegant Riley Park, which had, and still has, a cricket pitch. It had solid, small houses, and was a modest, affordable neighbourhood of families, seniors, students, and artists. Then, with its re-branding as Calgary's first revitalized inner-city neighbourhood, development struck, house prices soared, elderly people were bought out, infill housing proliferated, and density increased, still, however, within the general height limits of the original neighbourhood.

One of the anchors of Hillhurst-Sunnyside was the Plaza Theatre, a 1930s movie house that in the late 1970s was Calgary's only rep-cinema. It had a little plaza in front of it where two streets met at an odd angle. These streets also produced a flatiron site, which became a building called The Point, a three-storey classic postmodern project of the 1980s. It is a significant enough piece of architecture to validate the main street landscape of this neighbourhood.

One or two new significant building projects in what might be a pretty louche, shabby area will indicate that the area is worth investing in, that the area has the potential for sophisticated architecture and life styles. Such projects will allow a neighbourhood to turn a corner, to maintain its basic fabric without obliteration by redevelopment. In a social sense, it gives a neighbourhood a centre that is aspirational and optimistic. The other open, urban public space in this neighbourhood is in front of the Safeway — a vintage glulam, freespan 1960s grocery store with an LRT stop next to it and a plaza-like parking lot. Unlike The Point, the Safeway and LRT stop are utilities, necessities; they lack the frisson of frivolity, the invitation to *be* frivolous, which The Point offers.

A similar set of urban conditions can be found in Mission, a neighbourhood cluster between the Elbow River to the south and east 17th Avenue South and the escarpments that lead to Mount Royal to the west. Fourth Street, its main street, had a string of desultory services: the art-deco Tivoli theatre, a medical centre, various gas stations, a bicycle shop, a hardware store, and a Safeway — nothing too coherent until it, too, was discovered in the late 1970s, when it developed a restaurant row, and east of 4th Street, an increasingly dense apartment zone on the Elbow River.

There was a lot of pressure on Mission to redevelop to higher residential densities, which it has, in a fashion. The Holy Cross Hospital was closed and turned into apartments and condominiums; however, the value of each site on 4th Street quickly increased as an investment that could be flipped rather than as a commitment to the rebuilding of a coherent community. Many major plots, some occupying whole blocks, have sat empty and abandoned for years caught in some sort of real estate limbo.

Mission

In 2001 Jenkins Architecture designed a multi-use building called 4th Street Central for the site across from the Tivoli Theatre (no longer a theatre, the building still exists in its original form if not use). The project consisted of a base of retail on the street with offices above, topped with stacked townhouses. Two nine-story towers of what was described as luxury residential fulfilled density requirements. It was articulate enough as architecture, and complex enough as program to lock down the middle section of 4th Street, just where the building fabric starts to fracture into parking lots and isolated buildings.

Why projects don't happen is not always that they are wrong for their times; this is a case of a project aligned quite perfectly with its times. However, architecture is a profession blown about by economic insecurity. Good projects need good clients to recognize that architecture is more than a business opportunity it also contributes to the health and goodwill of the greater community. When fees are not paid and development permits not applied for, projects don't happen.

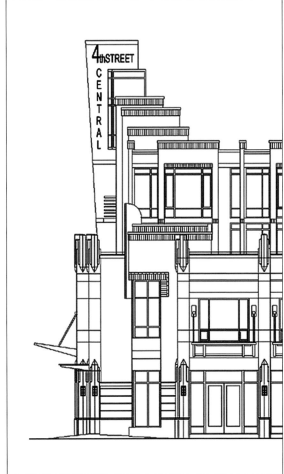

Figure 36-1. This project draws heavily on the original simple 1930 art-deco architecture of the Tivoli Theatre and then elaborates into a dense essay on late 1930s Egyptian style similar to some of Frank Lloyd Wright's work, such as his 1923 Hollyhock House in Los Angeles. If the jumping around in various eras is confusing here, it is because we are looking at a series of reiterations: Wright's homage to a kind of Hollywood Egypt as the Tutankhamen tomb was discovered; the Tivoli theatre's homage to 1920s Hollywood; Dan Jenkins's homage to the Tivoli itself and thus to all of its references.

Dan Jenkins Architects, Calgary, Alberta.

It isn't just the size of the project that is important here, it is also the architecture. These main streets are intimate, built at a 1910 scale when the road was full of horses, carts, bicycles, and feet. There were small stores with apartments above them, small industries such as the Palm Dairies once located at the top of 4th Street, or the chicken hatcheries that were on 9th Avenue in Inglewood up until the late 70s. The butchers, the bakers, the small-scale enterprises: this kind of micro-zoning is what, since the 1980s, we have desperately tried to replicate in new residential areas as the antithesis of the shopping mall. These key regeneration projects cannot be too tall or large, throwing the existing fabric into irrelevance, nor can they be too self-contained, which is the problem with any project that does not contribute to the street with retail on the sidewalk.

Inglewood

Henri's, in Inglewood, was a 1980s bar made out of an old 1950s atomic-styled gas station: all shooting roofs and too much pavement for 9th Avenue in its present neighbourhood main street incarnation. Just thirty years ago however, there were five service stations in a three-block stretch of 9th Avenue, three autobody shops, four car lots, a radiator repair garage, and a carwash. All the gas stations have gone; two are now city parking lots, one is a coffee shop, one is an empty lot of weeds and magpies (Henri's), the radiator place is a design studio and gallery, and the carwash and transmission garage are buried under a new block-long mixed-use development that includes the Esker Gallery. We quickly forget how scrappy these inner-city neighbourhood streets were when they were not in fashion. The last thirty years has seen an infilling of the street wall, eliminating uses and buildings that no longer conform to the millennial view of a coherent, resolutely pedestrianized urban streetscape.

The Henri's site, on the corner of 9th Avenue and 13th Street, is zoned DC, or Direct Control, which means, effectively, "propose something." The 2004 design proposition by Rick Balbi Architects is a mixed-use seven-storey project, set back marginally from the sidewalk with a small courtyard on the back alley. Three different facades were proposed, each with a retail ground floor, four middle floors of apartments with inset balconies, and a set back penthouse level on the top. It is proposed in red brick, forming a set piece with the 1910 Gresham Block across the street to the east. Just one block south is another set piece, the 1912 red-brick Sevenoaks Apartments on the west side of 13th Street with the 1911 St. Andrews church across the street to the east. The next block south has the old red-brick-coloured pressed-tin Hudson's Bay Warehouse, now studios, on the west side, and a 1990s townhouse project on the east side. Each block repeats this quite unusual urban sequence. The Henri's site is key to fulfilling the procession.

The site itself has some contamination issues, having been a service station, and by being so close to the Bow River, water is found at twelve feet down. The provision of underground parking was quite expensive; the developer-builder decided not to continue, then reconsidered the parking and decided to continue, but in the intervening delay, the owners of the land themselves decided to do something else, and put the site up for sale, where it has remained empty and fenced-off since.

The site will be developed, and it will follow the lines of this 2004 proposal — all urban logic points this way.

Inner-City Neighbourhood Main Streets [179]

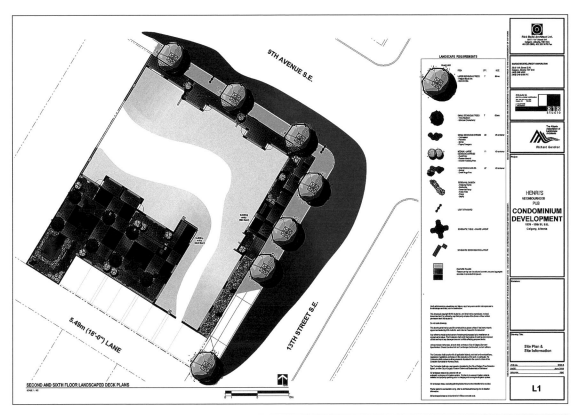

Figure 36-2. What doesn't show in this perspective and plan is the landscape of small houses squeezed between 9th Avenue and the light industrial warehouses that flank the CPR tracks. This is one of the oldest neighbourhoods in Calgary, built for CPR workers and correspondingly humble in scale. The inevitable development of the corner site at 9th Avenue and 13th Street Southeast applies pressure on its immediate hinterland to densify, replacing small bungalows with two-and-a-half-storey infills.
Rick Balbi Architect, Calgary, Alberta.

HOUSING AND DENSIFICATION

Chapter 37

Densification

In Bill Milne's files in the Provincial Archives are a number of 1950s slab apartment towers resting on horizontal plinths, so many that they become a motif. The plinth floats above the ground plane, invariably one end covers a driveway, and the towers are narrow and plain. The contrast between the vertical apartment and the horizontal base, whether it be lobby and porte-cochère, or as in figure 37-1, an office for Western Union, keeps the height of the project low at the street edge.

In the 2010s perimeter block housing proposed for the East Village, the residential component is also an apartment block over a plinth of commercial or retail (figure 37-2), but they are not formally separate pieces. Balbi's proposal for Henri's site also follows this model: the street wall sits on the sidewalk from base to top.

In between these two models, the point block apartment building and the main street perimeter block, there was kind of densification that loaded the site with

Figure 37-1. W.G. Milne, Western Union Office and Apartment Block. n.d.

W.G. Milne fonds, Provincial Archives of Alberta.

Figure 37-2. Alternative facade for the 9th Avenue development on the Henri's site.
Rick Balbi Architect, Calgary, Alberta.

townhouses at the base and apartment towers above set back from the street wall, opening up the street to more light while maintaining a townhouse scale of development with a very high density.

THE BELTLINE

One such housing project, designed in 1982 during the second oil boom, was proposed for the Beltline district, a zone in south west Calgary just south of the CPR line that consists of a mix of single family residential, three-storey walk-up apartment blocks, and medium- to high-rise apartment towers. Ron Boruk's project, Connaught Estates, has a four-storey base of interlocking townhouse units, a hybrid of the house and the apartment, that all have direct street access.

Calgary did not develop the apartment block tradition found in Winnipeg or Toronto. Other than a few significant 1900s blocks such as the Lorraine or the Devenish, half a dozen brick terraces dating from 1910, and a scattering of 1930s to 1950s three-storey twelve-unit walk ups that could fit on two residential side-by-side lots, single-family houses have long been Calgary's norm. The modernist horizontal slabs of the Spruce Cliff Apartments, built in 1954 just north of the Shaganappi Golf Course, were a startling response to the post–Second World War housing crisis in Calgary that resulted from European immigration, returning veterans who were too old and too experienced to return to the houses of their parents, and the delayed marriages held over from both the Depression and the war. Most often apartments were treated as way stations while saving for a house mortgage. The 1960s saw the development of seven- to twelve-storey apartment towers throughout the Beltline, building a significant pool of housing within a few blocks of the burgeoning downtown core. A similar condition, and one which most Calgarians would have been familiar with at the time, is Vancouver's West End, a large residential district that after the Second World War began to replace old houses with walk-ups, then towers, and now very tall condominiums. This strategy, densification of the inner city, is a foil to suburban expansion at the edges of the city.

In the late 1970s when downtown was covered with cranes and office towers under construction, and there was pressure for residential construction to keep up, vacancy rates were near zero, housing was in short supply, house prices were highly inflated, and mortgages were between 17 to 24 percent. Connaught Estates, similar to many projects of the late 1970s and early 80s, was a hybrid multi-family housing project that maintained the historic relationship of single-family house to street while stacking the site with an apartment tower set

DENSIFICATION [185]

Figure 37-3. Architectural drawings, whether perspectives or elevations, show every detail, implying a building that looks more complex than it ever does in reality where an overall impression to someone passing by is much more general. The basic form here is of an apartment building, with balconies and a stepped-back base. It keeps the street open, providing a separation between the road and sidewalk and the apartment stack. Indications of planted roof decks and balconies is optimistic: climate works against this in practice, but one is always hopeful.

Ron Boruk Architects, Calgary, Alberta.

back in the site. It avoided streets as apartment block-lined canyons: the high density zoned for the area was ameliorated by the stepped-back base. The project also avoided the anonymity of conventional apartment lobby after apartment lobby that do not make welcoming street environments. Jane Jacobs's valorization of "eyes on the street," written about in *The Life and Death of Great American Cities*, and her subsequent move to Toronto as a "liveable city" were tremendously influential in Calgary at the level of Area Redevelopment plans. Jacobs's thinking floods Connaught Estates: high density, lots of people around; 1,200-square-foot houses, not just apartments, and therefore the presence of children; front doors close to the sidewalk; friendly surveillance and community-building. And this was openness not just at street level. Circulation elements such as lobbies, the transitional amenity floor between townhouses and apartments, and especially the stairwells in the apartment block were transparent and made safer by being so.

Like almost every project developed in 1981 meant to be built in 1982, financing was approved and then the client sold the property as the housing market crashed along with the crash in Alberta's oil exploration and investment sector. Eventually, a version of these townhouses were built in Banff, minus the apartment tower. The particular hybrid model of different housing types in one project didn't come around again when the market picked up. On the Connaught Estates site, two-storey townhouses were eventually built, the packed density of the earlier proposal no longer as desirable as it had been in the early 1980s.

Nonetheless, densification is a constant discussion in the neighbourhoods close to downtown. The models continue to change, however. The next project, for laneway housing in Mission, shows another strategy.

Chapter 38

Laneway Houses

In 2007 there was an active debate in Calgary about secondary suites, basement suites, granny flats, and converted garages. Unless zoned specifically R-2, they were illegal. In 2008 the City of Calgary developed secondary suite guidelines, including laneway housing — small units whose access is from the alley, or lane, built in the backyards of single houses on standard lots. The minimum house size of one thousand square feet also had to be relaxed, given that often the existing houses in the inner city neighbourhoods where laneway housing was proposed were already less than the required one thousand square feet. There was great opposition to this kind of densification; sardines were usually invoked in the press along with loss of privacy, loss of the backyard for the kids, and increased traffic.

Planning standards set out in zoning regulations have two goals: "To ensure development in a given area is consistent, and to ensure that development matches available infrastructure and environmental services." Specified are lot dimensions, setbacks, and the area covered by building and building height. In a report to the City of Calgary about Smart Growth, Tomalty and Haider point out that this can lead to architectural monotony and prevent socio-economic diversity.[1] Planning standards can insist on houses larger than needed and on single-storey houses covering most of the lot (instead of a multi-storey house covering just a corner of a lot). To increase housing affordability, these standards must change. Smaller lots reduce land costs and the length of utilities per dwelling. Decreasing lot coverage also reduces the allowable size of a house to something more affordable.

Dividing the lot, or severance, depending on the configuration of the lot, can be done either side by side

---

1 Tomalty and Haider, *Housing Affordability and Smart Growth in Calgary*, p. 175–77.

or front to back. For the front to back division, which would allow the laneway house, minimum street frontage must be relaxed, as well as the setback from the back property line, and lane frontage has to be allowed. The 2008 Land Use Bylaws included R-IN: single-detached houses on minimum 233-square-metre lots, 7.5-metre frontage, and 60 percent coverage. This roughly equals the standard 25-foot lot that is found in the early twentieth-century inner city, indicating that the density of inner-city fabric is what more spacious subdivisions could be considering. A 2004 study showed that only 11 percent of Calgary's houses were in the old Land Use Bylaw R-1A, RS-1, or RS-2 zones. Current zoning allows a laneway house if the lot is 13 metres wide and 400 square metres in area. This indicates lots that are 43 feet wide and 102 feet deep, the kind of lot found in the postwar suburbs built in the late 1950s, including Chinook Park, Haysboro, Acadia, Charleswood, Lakeview, and Varsity, and these are the kinds of neighbourhoods most resistant to the very concept of densification.

New Urbanism developments such as Garrison Woods, Garrison Green, and McKenzie Towne have laneway housing or, as it goes under various names, garden and garage suites. These are, however, part of a different housing ethos than individual infill development, where a small intense unit, space efficient and affordable, could be built in the backyard of a sprawling 1958 split-level ranch house in Chinook Park. Garrison Woods and Garrison Green, for example, were developed en masse from old Canadian Forces housing at Currie Barracks re-zoned as Direct Control, using New Urbanism guidelines for a more dense, more diverse, more intimate neighbourhood fabric than the older surrounding 1950s and 60s suburbs, which have the lowest densities of all. It is this belt, close to downtown, which needs densification, and laneway housing is instead increasingly proposed for already compact inner-city neighbourhoods and for new community development on the edge of Calgary, intensifying population at the far reaches of the transportation network, increasing traffic on the highways and feeder routes.

Gerald Forseth Architects, in 2002, much earlier than the heated discussion about laneway infill and granny flats in backyards, proposed a serious intensification of the block between 23rd and 24th Avenues Southwest and 4th Street in the Mission district. This block has a lane, retail at its west end and a 1915 two-storey brick apartment building at the east end. This leaves twelve two-and-a-half-storey wood frame houses built in 1911 on twenty-five foot lots. The proposal was to build a wall of condominium units across the backyards of the house lots; four storeys on the south side of the lane, six storeys on the north. The backyards of the existing houses would be excavated to provide parking accessible from the half alley behind the retail on 4th Street. The existing houses would be linked with the new condominiums by paved courtyards above the underground parking.

This was a radical yet supremely logical proposal that gives us a position from which to consider the much more serendipitous plans for Smart Growth policy (fiscally, socially, and environmentally responsible land use and development) and individual lot-by-lot densification. This project asks us to retain old wheat and real estate boom Calgary — tall, capacious wood houses with porches and attics — as a streetscape, keeping the street's front yard trees and its intimacy, while optimizing the alley by lining it with thin walls of living units, accessible by elevator and stairs reached through the courtyards. Streets are preserved and the alleys, usually dusty, littered and full of blue and black

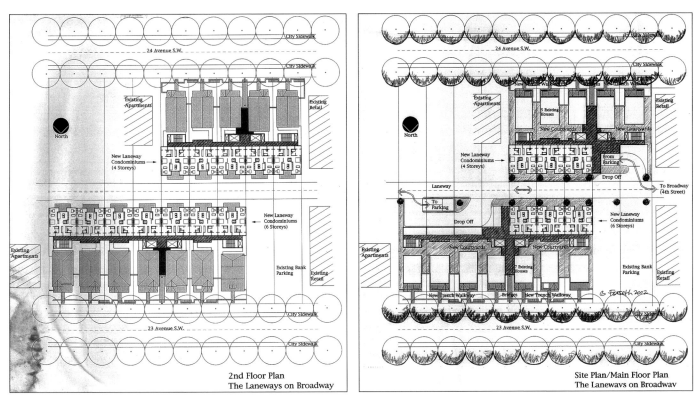

Figure 38-1. If one thinks of the basic ground-floor plan of any of the 1912 houses at the front of the lots — capacious, simple rooms — and the floor plans of the new condominiums, one can see how much of a scale change there is here. It is two different universes, with different furniture, different quality of light, different relationships between the inside rooms and the outside gardens or courtyards, a different spatiality entirely.

Gerald L. Forseth Architects, Calgary, Alberta.

bins, become an intimate canyon overlooked by balconies and decks of the proportions we all like to visit on holidays in other, older, more sociable cities such as Lisbon or Barcelona. The point isn't that we should ape Europe, but rather we can make the city more liveable by increasing the number of people that live within a block of the neighbourhood main streets throughout the inner city. These older neighbourhoods could be razed of course, as happened with Victoria Park, and replaced by residential towers rising from mixed-use retail and office plinths — the Vancouver model. Victoria Park is an increasingly exciting urban corner of Calgary, attracting a young, sophisticated demographic that wants to live right downtown. Mission, however, or Inglewood, or Bridgeland, draw much of their charm from their generally humble beginnings, their affordability, and their fulfillment of a nostalgia for small towns within the city.

Forseth developed this proposal for the City of Calgary as a demonstration project for intensification of a heritage area that was unlikely to survive further development pressure associated with future building booms. It had support from the planning department and the alderman of the area at the time, Madeleine King, who was defeated in the election that occurred shortly after. Three other large housing projects nearby, which had knocked down several blocks of historic houses, had run into financial difficulties and construction had halted, so the impetus to continue the laneway project fell away. In the intervening years, infill development has changed as well. Rather than new block-sized multi-family townhouse complexes to which the laneway project was meant as an alternative, smaller townhouse projects with less capital investment and on smaller sites have become the norm. The community Area Redevelopment Plan encourages smaller scale piecemeal projects and the heritage landscape from the 1911 Calgary real estate boom remains unprotected, gently mouldering away, the old houses falling one by one.

This all raises a question about possible densification of the low-density postwar 1960s suburbs: they don't have adjacent retail streets; instead, they have shopping centres to which one must drive. Suburban densification would increase traffic because, unlike densification in the inner city, where amenities are in the next block, in the curving crescents and cul-de-sacs of postwar suburbia, there is nowhere to walk to.

Chapter 39

The Scale of Houses Between 1955 and 1975

We tend to think that densification is a contemporary concern as we try to re-urbanize a city built largely to suburban standards through the last half of the twentieth century. It is sometimes salutary to remind ourselves that before the advent of the 1980s monster house with its monster furniture, double height entry, and triple garage, suburban houses weren't that large. Here are two unbuilt houses from the late 1950s (figure 39-1) and one triplex from the mid 1970s (39-2).

The thin little 930-square-foot house on a 45-foot-wide lot, stamped by Lloyd French when he was working with Beatson Finlayson Architects, has two bedrooms, one bathroom, and the kitchen right at the front, near the front door. Bedroom closets are three by six feet, and that is for a couple — today it would hardly hold the couples shoes. Rather than the living room facing the street, as is usual, here the living room is in the centre of the house and faces into the side yard. From the elevations, this house appears to be squeezed between two three-storey walk-up apartments and presents a quite shuttered aspect to the street. This kind of domesticity is almost inaccessible today, yet, in the newest of downtown condos, such as Batistella's Colours, say, the living units are just as spare and minimal, stacked into a thirty-storey building. In the intervening fifty years, house sizes ballooned, peaked, and now, with rising energy costs, are shrinking again.

The next sketch is for a 1,300-square-foot house on a 66-by-114-foot lot. From its size, one can see that this is not an inner-city lot but rather a lot found in the 1950s subdivisions such as Marlborough or Chinook Park. These projects are all single-sheet sketch drawings with no addresses or clients; today, it is almost impossible to either locate them or know why they were done. What is interesting is how they present a family and that family's

[192]   Unbuilt Calgary

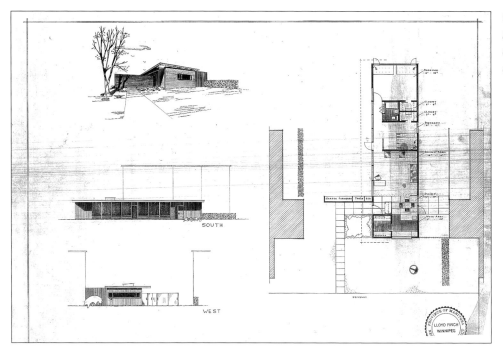

Figure 39-1.
Narrow Lot House. Beatson Finlayson Fonds. Canadian Architectural Archives, University of Calgary. 121A/82.6, BEA 00H68.

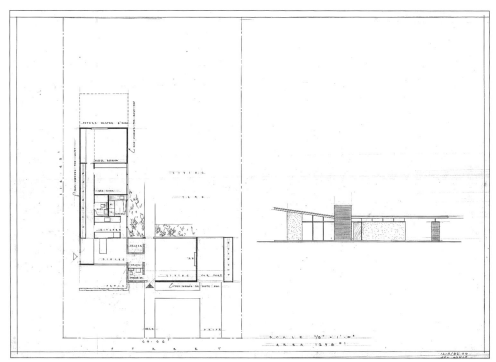

Figure 39-2.
House, Beatson Finlayson Fonds. Canadian Architectural Archives, University of Calgary 121A/82.6, BEA 00H68.

relationship to the neighbours. This house does not have a window on the street; the living room looks into the backyard (although it has "high windows for south sun" on the front), the powder room is windowless, and the dining room looks out onto an external patio room, shielded from the street by a proposed hedge. The house could extend, linearly, to the end of the lot, adding bedroom after bedroom. Like French's house, the backyard is at the side of the house, here labelled "living yard." It is all terribly protective: the lot itself was conceived of as a living room, private and shielded by the house. No garage, just a carport.

Beatson's triplex (figure 39-3) dates probably from the early to mid-1970s and starts to show a stacking of the site. This is an amalgamation of three twenty-five-foot lots, which indicates it is in the old inner city, in this case on 15th Street and 37th Avenue Southwest. There are two two-storey units and one little 670-square-foot unit at the end, squeezed into half a lot because of an easement. The triplex is built upon a hill, and the change in grade is absorbed by a central atrium, the stairs, and a solid wall between bath and kitchen (or bath and toilet in the middle unit). Closet space has doubled from our two earlier houses, there are more toilets, and the kitchens are smaller, so small in the tiny unit as to be probably unusable unless one lived out of a microwave. How standards change. Although these three designs are in the archives as unbuilt sketches, they were typical of their times, and something similar would have been built all over the city.

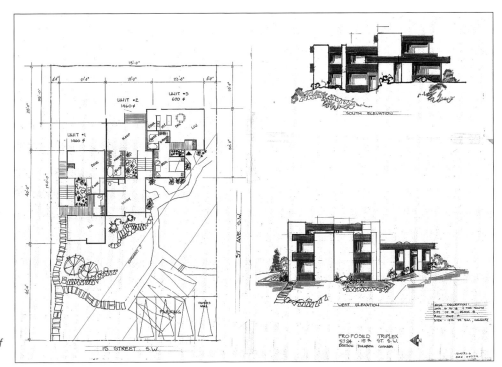

Figure 39-3.
Proposed Triplex, Beatson Finlayson fonds, Canadian Architectural Archives, University of Calgary. 121A/82.6, BEA 00T74.

In 1967 the then Central Mortgage Housing Corporation (CMHC) commissioned a series of experimental housing projects across Canada. The units were to be affordable for lower-income families, and the CMHC would facilitate purchase. This departed from much CMHC housing, which was, usually, townhouse complexes of rental units. In northeast Calgary, areas such as Rundle and Pengrove are classic CMHC landscapes. Jack Long did a very interesting proposal for Pengrove (see figures 39-4 to 39-7) that specified that the front and backyard setbacks be the only open space, with a split level house in between, so everything was as minimal as possible but still within the liveable standards of both CMHC and City of Calgary setbacks. This project was built, and sits on 52nd Street Southeast just south of Memorial Drive as a kind of demonstration project of an extremely interesting residential landscape. The investment in such a scheme was meant to be replicated where needed throughout the city, which it wasn't, as while Canada was in a recession in the late 1960s and early 1970s, the OPEC crisis of 1973–74 propelled intense exploration and development in the oil sands, starting Calgary's second oil-fuelled boom. Houses, even low-income houses, responded expansively. The Pengrove demonstration stood for a more desperate and a more frugal time. Where this project offers much to contemporary urbanism is in the discussion of laneway houses, which are, by definition, tiny and squeezed into a rear-yard setback. We are entering an era of cutbacks, downsizing, and streamlining. This proposal shows a way to build a small community of small houses, conserving land, embedded energy, and materials.

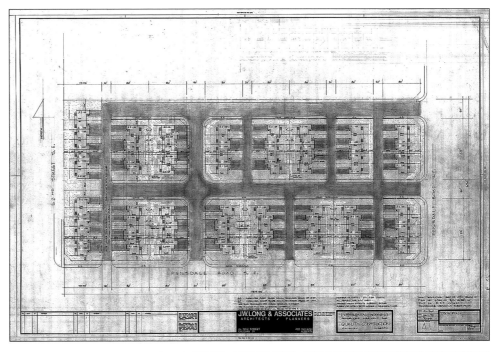

Figure 39-4.

Pembroke Meadows, Jack Long fonds, Canadian Architectural Archives, University of Calgary. 12A/77.55, LON 7006.

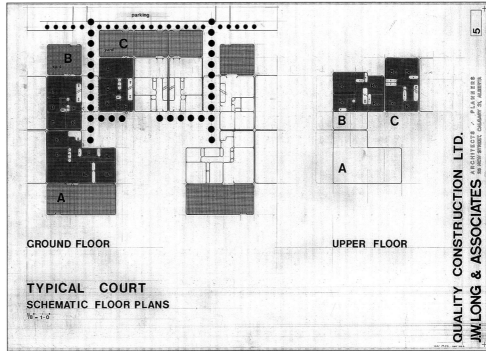

Figure 39-5.

Pembroke Meadows, Jack Long fonds, Canadian Architectural Archives, University of Calgary. 12A/77.55, LON 7006.

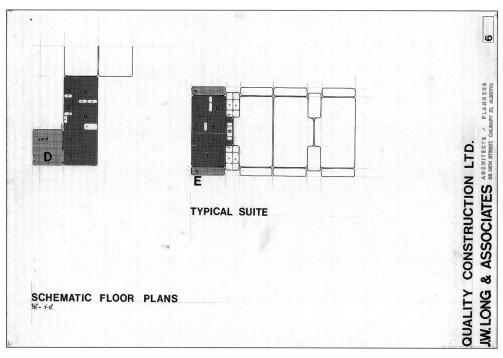

Figure 39-6.

Pembroke Meadows, Jack Long fonds, Canadian Architectural Archives, University of Calgary. 12A/77.55, LON 7006.

Figure 39-7.

Pembroke Meadows, Jack Long fonds, Canadian Architectural Archives, University of Calgary. 12A/77.55, LON 7006.

STAMPEDE GROUNDS

Chapter 40

The Stampede in a Regional Context

It is difficult to find anything new to say about the Stampede, as so much powerful material has been written about it. But one cannot consider Calgary without including the Stampede, especially its beginnings as an agricultural exhibition.

Just two years after the CPR line between Halifax and Vancouver was completed, in 1884, the Calgary and District Agricultural Society held its first fair, continuing each year until 1894, when the society was disbanded. It was reactivated as the Inter-Western Pacific Exhibition Company in 1899 and in 1910 renamed the Calgary Industrial Exhibition Company, a name it held until 1933. The rodeo connection was made in 1912, by Guy Weadick, an American promoter, and although the Calgary Exhibition and Stampede is a name that dates only from 1956, stampede events have been held in conjunction with the Calgary Exhibition since 1923.

In 1950, Calgary built the Stampede Corral, the largest arena in Canada west of Toronto. By 1980 and the acquisition of the Calgary Flames, this arena no longer met NHL standards; however, it wasn't until 1984 that the 1988 Winter Olympics propelled the building of the Saddledome. Before this, however, in 1964, there had been a plan to move the Stampede grounds away from its impacted site in Victoria Park on the Elbow River. A site at Lincoln Park, the disused airfield near Currie Barracks, was proposed and received both federal and city approval. It was, however, vigorously opposed by surrounding communities and the Stampede stayed in Victoria Park, initiating a forty-five year campaign to slowly remove the Victoria Park neighbourhood, a process which is now complete except for a small handful of holdout houses. Even the name, Victoria Park, named after Queen Victoria, who was still alive when the community was formed, has been superseded by the more general Beltline East and the Rivers District, a redevelopment area that stretches the length of the south side of the CPR railway line and the west side of the Elbow River.

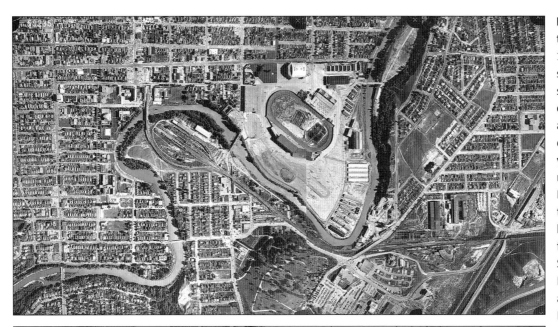

Figure 40-1. This aerial of the stampede grounds in 1961, with Victoria Park still in place, shows how small the site was. Plans to expand into Lindsay Park, across the river, depended on the removal of the CNR yards, and in the end did not happen. The Lindsay Park Sports Centre, now the Talisman Centre, was built on this site in 1983 for the Western Canada Summer Games. Victoria Park was clearly the only area suitable for expansion. Directly south of the Stampede is Cemetery Hill, a steep cliff faces it to the east, and to the west was an immovable industrial object, so to the north it went.
Hunting Survey Corporation, air photo files from MADGIC, University of Calgary.

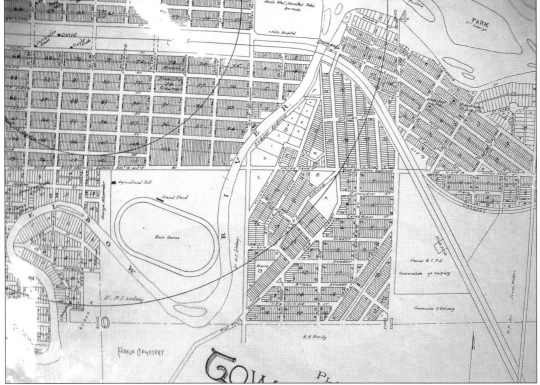

Figure 40-2. In 1911, Dr. N.J. Lindsay owned the land in the quarter section that the race track was on and had proposed development of the other loop in the Elbow River that was eventually sold to the CNR.
Courtesy of the Calgary Public Library, Community Heritage and Family History Collection

Max Foran has written about the long and complex relationship between the City of Calgary and the Stampede Board, often contentious, riven by rivalries and jurisdictional disputes, the intertwining of aldermen and board members, conflicts of interest — it is a long story. What we might do here is consider how Calgary would have been different had the Stampede relocated to Lincoln Park. During the Second World War, a branch of the Provincial Technology Institute (now known as SAIT) had been located on the Stampede site in Victoria Park. When in 1964 it was proposed that the Stampede go to Lincoln Park and that Mt. Royal College, also bidding for the ex-airfield, move into the Stampede Grounds in Victoria Park, it was actually the resurrection of a much older idea. However, 1964 was a period of powerful suburban expansion all around the edges of the city. An urban Mount Royal College would have been similar to Ryerson in Toronto, established in 1948 as Ryerson Institute of Technology, inheriting the property and infrastructure of the previous Toronto Normal School. For Calgary, however, in the middle of the first oil boom, a downtown higher education facility would not have been seen as advanced thinking but as just another project that would increase congestion in the inner-city neighbourhoods, none of which were especially prestigious.

In the intervening sixty years, it has become desirable for suburban universities to have downtown branches, recognizing that the urban environment opens up contacts between academia and the public, if nothing else. Twentieth-century university models, however, isolated universities from downtown cores, as seen with the University of Regina in Wascana Park, the University of British Columbia on its vast grounds, the University of Calgary on its extensive grounds in northwest Calgary, or, as it turned out, Mount Royal University located deep in the southwest of the city, served by Glenmore and Crowchild Trails but not well-served by public transit.

Had the Stampede relocated to Lincoln Park, which had recently been decommissioned in 1963, adjacent to Currie Barracks (decommissioned in 1998), and despite the opposition of the Lakeview Community, an up-market subdivision with lake and golf course, it would today form part of a large district of open land and barracks where events at the scale of Cirque du Soleil performances are held. With the turning of Currie Barracks over to Canada Lands, a federal body that develops federal land holdings for new uses — usually housing — the Stampede would have been surrounded on its east and south sides by dense neighbourhoods as it is in its present and original location, but with much more room to expand. In 1960 the Stampede had tried to expand into Lindsay Park, across MacLeod Trail, where old marshalling yards for the Canadian National Railway had been. This land was expensive and surrounding properties needed consolidation. Lincoln Park, on the other hand, was not expensive and was already a single package of land that didn't need an amalgamation of individual land holders.

Max Foran explains the process of losing Lincoln Park as a battle of wills and purposes between the Stampede Board, City Hall, and the Lakeview community — political and financial all the way. To add to this is the larger perception of the shape of Calgary as an efficiently zoned modern city and how that was to be maintained. The Stampede was simply a week-long Old West celebration, its location in the original grazing pastures of the NWMP Fort Calgary, was tucked away in a corner of the city that was not valued for new residential construction. It was in the same quadrant of the city as all the Burns industries — the stockyards, the feed mills, cattle, horses, and cowboys. There is a historic logic to this site that was missing from the Lincoln Park location.

Figure 40-3. In this circa 1940 map, the size of the racetrack appears to have shrunk from its 1911 size, and clearly typed on the site is Institute of Technology, Victoria Park, possibly a wartime training facility.

Map of the City of Calgary, printed for the Hudson's Bay Company. A.P. van Buren, Calgary, circa 1940. Community Resources, the Calgary Public Library.

Chapter 41

Stampede Accessibility

For almost fifty years, the Stampede grounds were sited between two Grand Trunk and Pacific Railway terminals. Lindsay Park, which on the 1911 map was subdivided into house lots, was soon thereafter bought by Grand Trunk (later the Canadian National Railway), still in operation in the 1961 aerial photograph of the Stampede grounds. Fort Calgary itself had been acquired by the Grand Trunk Pacific Railway in 1914 for a rail terminal. MacCosham's had a warehouse on the site, and in 1969 an archaeological survey was conducted by the University of Calgary to find the old fort, which they did, under a storage yard. The City of Calgary bought the land in 1974, and reconstruction of the original 1875 palisade fort and a later 1888 NWMP barracks began. Since then, the wide fields, replanted as short-grass prairie, are where the hundreds of horses for the Stampede Parade muster each year. The site is transformed by horse trailers, camps, and corrals, which take this ancient and important land south of the Bow and west of the Elbow back to its very origins.

The Stampede grounds are held in a loop of the Elbow River and bordered on the west side by MacLeod Trail and to the north by the CPR main line. It also uses a narrow strip of land on the east side of the Elbow River, underneath the sandstone escarpment that forms the west edge of Ramsay, for horse barns. The site is so impacted and so dense that every scrap of land is put to use. The corner by the 1913 MacDonald Bridge is now simply used as a private entrance to the horse barns; however, its longer history was of a campground. In 1940 the Sunshine Auto Court applied for a building permit to turn the campsite into something more permanent, proposing a store, a kitchen, a toilet, shower and laundry building, three areas for tents, one for trailers, and lots of cabins, singles, doubles, and five-unit rows. A campsite was consistent with the use of riverbanks in Calgary up

[204] Unbuilt Calgary

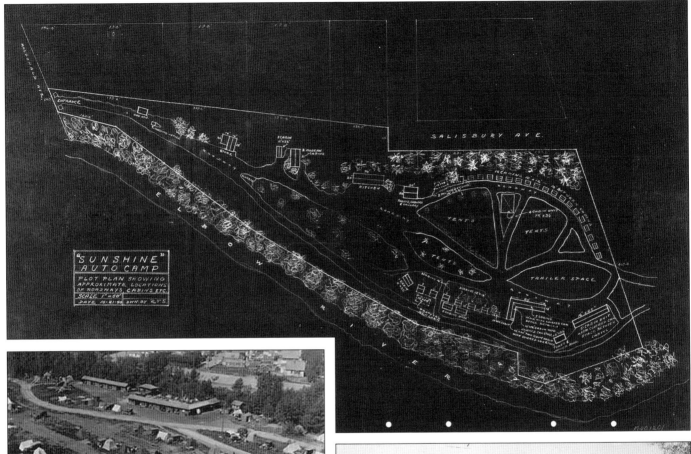

Figure 41-1. The proposal for the Sunshine Auto Court for a development permit from the city is much more organized than it was in reality, formalizing a campsite that had existed almost as long as Calgary itself. The photograph of campsites on St. George's Island shows how natural they were.

Clockwise: courtesy of Corporate Records and Archives, City of Calgary; courtesy of Library and Archives Canada; courtesy of the Calgary Public Library, Community Heritage and Family History Collection.

until the 1950s. The shift to renaming it an auto court merely acknowledged that things were looking up, although in 1940 this seems a bit premature. Like the islands in the Bow River with their picnic grounds and campsites, the Sunshine Auto Court site proposed lightweight construction in a fragile riverine ecology. Plus, it was right at the edge of the Stampede. There is an intense feeling of easy accessibility in these early spatial geographies of the Stampede, which today is completely absent.

Mawson

The Mawson plan includes a formal layout for Victoria Park Exhibition Grounds on the current Stampede site. Symmetrical and formal buildings, a new horse show building, grandstands, sale rooms, a concert hall, and a large bandstand were all arrayed on an axis at forty-five degrees to Calgary's existing orthogonal street grid. The river is flanked by promenades; a major internal roadway separating the bandstand from the rest of the grounds leads on one side to the CNR depot and on the other to the Grand Trunk Pacific Railway depot — auspicious connections to Calgary's rural ranching hinterland.

While the layout of the Stampede Grounds might appear haphazard today, Mawson's diagonal interface with the city remains.

Chandler Kennedy Analysis

In 1984 Chandler Kennedy analyzed the agricultural complex of the Stampede Grounds with a series of studies that, on appearance, suggest that the grounds could be urbanized — that is, buildings could be located to improve orientation and legibility. These studies were done after the placing of the Saddledome and show a general aligning of adjacent buildings to the racetrack and a central focus to the rest of the grounds, looking away from the racetrack. The formality owes as much to an early 1980s architectural interest in classicism as it does to the Mawson plan; both eras eschewed the provisional and the informal, for different reasons perhaps, but with the same results: a turn to highly ordered planning defined by avenues of trees and hedging, representing a late Victorianism that appears still very civilized.

———

The Stampede Grounds are complex. The Stampede is an annual exhibition, as it was in Mawson's plan, and it is also a western event. It is on the rodeo circuit that stretches down to the Mexican border and has its own ranching-derived spatiality. It is also a performance space, and it has to have a midway. It has the Tipi Village, not as an exhibition but as a working relationship between the First Nations of southern Alberta and the Stampede. It contains the Country Music Hall of Fame and Nashville North, which for a long time were isolated pavilions surrounded by parking. In 2006 the Stampede announced it was going to begin to replace asphalt with parkland as part of the larger Rivers District study, to make the exhibition grounds truly a park, consistent with reducing the environmental footprint and preserving the banks of the Elbow River

The dilemma with the Stampede is that it is a ten-day festival that attracts several million visitors, and the rest of the year has a series of events that only use one or another of the large halls at any one time. During the hockey season, the Saddledome sells out for every game, and it is also the venue for rock concerts. Stampede Casino has daily use. The Big Four exhibit hall schedules the Home Show and the Boat Show — standard exhibition events. There are conferences. There are horse-related events, shows,

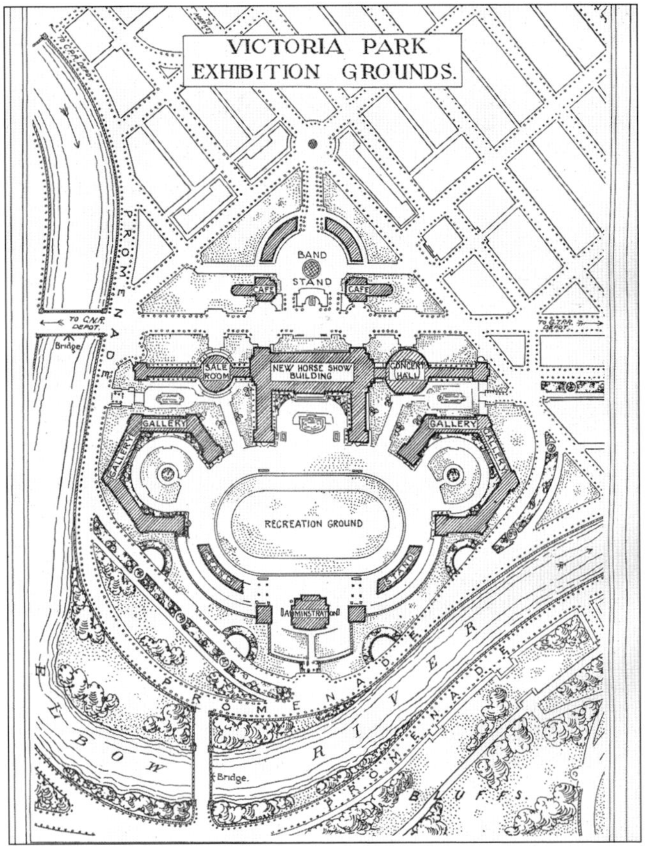

Figure 41-2. Mawson's formal plan for the Stampede Grounds — not to be called that for another dozen years, however — introduced the strong 45 degree orientation to all the buildings and the racetrack, something seen today still in the chamfered 45 degree corner of the BMO Centre at 12th and MacLeod Trail.
Courtesy of Canadian Architectural Archives, University of Calgary.

Figure 41-3. Although nothing else survives from the Mawson Plan for the Stampede Grounds, the 45-degree angle has. Note that the race track in this 1956 photograph is slightly misaligned. Mawson's intention, faced with a relentless orthogonal grid, was to choose significant projects, such as the Exhibition Grounds, and to break the grid in those locations so they would stand out as special.
Calgary Stampede Historical Committee.

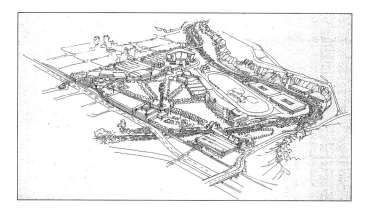

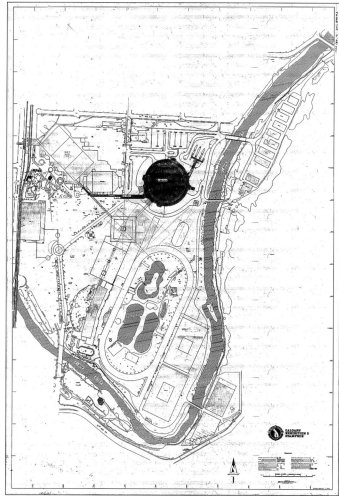

Figure 41-4. Note that the racetrack has been relocated and realigned. The Sunshine Auto Camp is gone, replaced by horse barns. The old 45 degree remains only in the Round Up Centre. The Saddledome has become a pivotal point. The re-introduction of some semblance of formal organization to what has become a fairly haphazard array of disparate large buildings shows in another pivot point near the Big Four building, with an orientation tower and radiating avenues leading to it.

Dale Chandler Kenedy fonds. Canadian Architectural Archives, University of Calgary. 195A/84.16, DAL 84002.

and races throughout the year; however, it is only during the Stampede that the whole site is activated. The most recent building, the BMO Centre, which has extended the Roundup Centre out to the corner of MacLeod Trail and 12th Avenue, presents a formal facade to the city, not unlike, in intention, Mawson's proposal. Both can be compared with the 1956 photograph of the old northwest corner on 15th Avenue with palisade gates and the Tipi Village right behind it. The Tipi Village is now on the southeast corner, a much quieter site on the Elbow River, and the northeast entrance is a display of contemporary architecture as befits the high-rise density of condominium and wine bar plans of east Beltline. Gradually, over the years, the Stampede has corporatized, leaving the flavour of the Old West behind, seen when the Round-Up Centre was renamed the BMO Centre.

This, too, is Calgary's dilemma, in that the Stampede is almost pure nostalgia: Calgary is an oil and gas supercity. The role of the Stampede was, and still is, a zone for letting go. Like any festival that involves costumes, one can lose one's everyday identity and sink into what normally would be transgressive behaviour but which, briefly, is sanctioned by the festival. The danger with the Stampede's architecture becoming conventional and integrated with the downtown commercial and new residential environment is that wild behaviour is not absorbed by old rough-and-ready palisades and endearingly hokey wild west buildings, signs, or scrap wood false fronts. Stampede behaviour, strictly social, is increasingly enacted in the controlled and contained physical environment that is downtown Calgary.

Does a city need a territory that allows decompression from a very fast-paced, live-hard life? Officially this kind of space is in the extensive park system, the bicycle paths, and the river parks. The red-light district and its associated bars in east Calgary have been redeveloped into the East Village, an arts and urban living district. Future plans for the Stampede grounds are threaded into the park system, featuring less parking and more parkland. Understandably, it makes for a safer and potentially more beautiful downtown core. The Stampede story and its current urban transformations signal that it is important that the event remain as part of Calgary's historic narrative but that it become as sophisticated as Calgary's other oil and gas narrative.

This section started with the 1964–65 plan to relocate the Stampede to a suburban site with much more land, not unlike the thinking that developed Heritage Park, where old buildings from both Calgary and surrounding small towns have been moved to a large park on the banks of the Glenmore Reservoir. After so much has been suburbanized — the universities, the heritage buildings, the markets, the cinemas, shopping, and artists — such a separation would not have allowed the Stampede with its Saddledome, its horse barns and races, its *essential history*, to continue to contribute to the richness of Calgary's downtown core.

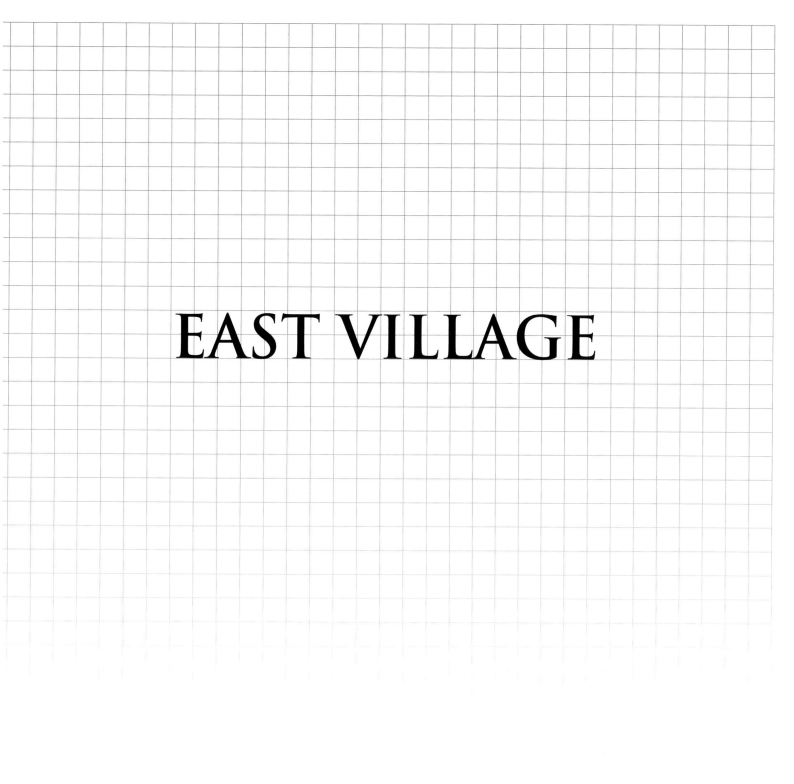

Chapter 42

Cantos Music Foundation and the King Edward Hotel

Close to the Stampede grounds and its expansion into Victoria Park — and the tall condo district cheek by jowl to the warehouses of 10th and 11th Avenues converted to IT companies and studios — is the East Village. The flagship project of the East Village is the Cantos Music Foundation, which has at its heart the King Edward Hotel, a small brick-and-sandstone hotel built in 1905, with more rooms added in 1910. It became a blues bar in the early 1980s, known as the King Eddy, and was headlined by blues acts of legend. It closed in 2004 and remained boarded up until 2011, when it underwent an asbestos and mould removal program. Facing the railway tracks, 9th Avenue East was once a string of small hotels and hotel bars that had long been notorious institutions — Calgary's version of Vancouver's East Hastings, but much shorter.

The King Edward Hotel's longer history has been obliterated by the clamour about the importance of the King Eddy blues bar. One of the traditions of the Calgary Highlanders Pipe Band was to finish up the Stampede Parade by breaking formation and marching single file, drums and bagpipes playing, into the King Eddy bar. Clearly, this pre-dates its blues bar standing. One reason the King Edward Hotel survived the urban renewal projects of the 1960s and 1980s was because of the ambiguous standing of the area between City Hall and the Elbow River, now known as East Village and Fort Calgary. Other than senior citizens marooned in three apartment buildings facing Fort Calgary, an experimental loft apartment block, and a row of townhouses, the area was rough, the purview of prostitutes, bikers, and indigents, an eyesore that eventually compelled the building of a large Salvation Army centre and hostel on 9th Avenue, and the Calgary Drop-In Centre, the downtown homeless shelter by the Cecil Hotel.

[212] UNBUILT CALGARY

Figure 42-1. This is Calgary at its most contradictory: the Stampede Parade with its thousands of horses assembled at Fort Calgary, the First Nations — from chiefs to babies, young boys riding bareback, buckskinned and beaded, the past Stampede Queens and their satinned and sequined horses, the visiting marching bands, the pipe bands, more horses, more First Nations, more bands, more horses — all marching through the glassy banking and energy industry towers of downtown, then past the Calgary Tower, past the Salvation Army Centre of Hope to the East Village and the Cantos National Music Centre, the end point of the parade.
Saucier + Perrotte Architects, Montreal.

Figure 42-2. The sense of a downtown performance stage covered, backed by reflective surfaces, intense and crowded, is a foil to sitting freezing in a summer thunderstorm at the folk festival in leafy Prince's Island Park. It also brings together the widely spread jazz venues in basements and borrowed art galleries of the struggling jazz festival.
Saucier + Perrotte Architects, Montreal.

Its new status is staggeringly different: the East Village, promoted as a desirable downtown residential district is anchored by three remaining historic buildings, the Cecil Hotel, the Simmons Mattress Factory, and the King Edward Hotel — none of which are particularly distinguished by anything other than their persistent longevity. The front facade and the corner neon sign of the King Edward Hotel now have historic designation protection; the rest of the building will be absorbed into the new Cantos Music Foundation centre, much in the way that the facade of the Burns Building was preserved in 1984 by absorbing the building into the Calgary Centre for Performing Arts.

The Cantos Music Foundation's National Music Centre building was determined by competition in 2009. The shortlisted five entries show an uneasy relationship with the King Edward Hotel. It reminds one strongly of the attitude to the City Hall in the Municipal Building Competition of 1981, where the older building hunkers small and cross in the corner of the site, while great architectural fireworks swoop about overhead. However, the King Edward is only one lens by which we can consider one of the more interesting proposals for the National Music Centre, the one by Saucier + Perrotte Architects from Montreal, which will remain unbuilt.

The Saucier + Perrotte proposal used the vernacular of contemporary downtown Calgary most beautifully, with smoked and clear glass transparencies, a monochromatic kind of commercial curtain wall construction. It seems ephemeral and lightweight, not that any building

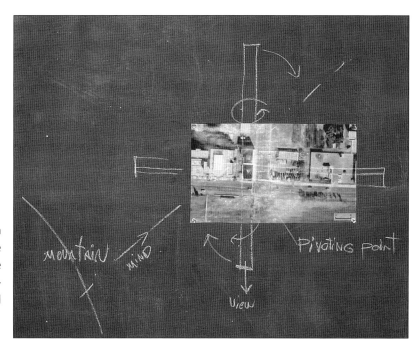

Figure 42-3. The important underlying factors in this project are laid out clearly here: the view of the mountains and the wind that comes from them, the site as a pivot in the city that takes the entire downtown which sits north-west of this King Edward and shoots its energy off to the south and the east.
Saucier + Perrotte Architects, Montreal.

can actually be either ephemeral or light weight. The appearance of wind and shadow is difficult to achieve, but this scheme does do that. Another proposal, by the French architect, Jean Nouvel, used a tall, slender slab of studios as a screen facing a lower building that acted as an amphitheatre. Dramatically scaled, Nouvel's project was a public demonstration of stage and audience; the scrim and the proscenium are the street. The Saucier + Perrotte proposal is less theatrical but has such strong echoes of the wind and ice of winter it would have reified the drama of Calgary's physical and environmental reality. Both proposals attempt to jolt the performing arts into public space rather than holding it within, as with the scheme chosen for the National Music Centre, designed by Allied Works of Portland, Oregon. This winning proposal is a much more solid, lapidary building with echoes of gleaming organ pipes at its rooftop. Both the Allied Works project and the 1984 Calgary Centre for Performing Arts present music and performance from within fortresses rather than from the public realm, something that was foregrounded in the Saucier + Perrotte proposal.

What is interesting here is how sometimes designers *not* involved in local imbroglios of City Hall, or media, or political histories see Calgary in landscape terms. In the Saucier + Perrotte proposal, the King Edward Hotel is made a significant point between the distant view of the mountains and the direct view of the CPR main line — it pivots the southwest context of Calgary into the East Village.

The competition brief for the $130 million centre included "honouring the iconic King Eddy Hotel while creating over 80,000 square feet of spectacular space that will house an education research centre, museum, world-renowned collection of instruments and memorabilia, recording studios, a radio station, a seven-days-a-week live music venue and a suite of innovative and creative programs for people of all ages." It is the presence of the King Edward Hotel here that tells much about contemporary Calgary and its relationship to its own history. Since the first oil boom of the 1960s, really significant architecture has been removed from the city, and what is left is often indifferent, overlooked because of accidents of location. Now, such relatively humble buildings are all Calgary has, and they are going to be sanctified no matter how inconvenient it will make future development.

The previous owner of the blues bar moved on to the Ironwood Blues Can in Inglewood. No doubt, it will move again, finding other free and relatively unfettered places to fit into. There will be a venue in the new music centre for blues to be played, but it won't be the kind of place that the King Eddy was, where unknowns played the same smoky stage as the greats. Culture is an evolutionary act — it doesn't stop changing. There must be places for development to take place, as well as technically advanced showcases for the already developed.

Chapter 43

EAST VILLAGE PLANS

We will end with a discussion of the East Village, that chunk of east downtown bounded by the Bow River, the Elbow, the CPR main line, the Municipal Building, and the Calgary Drop-In Centre. Through it runs the northeast and southwest LRT lines and several immutable features, including some 1960s senior citizens' slab apartments, Fort Calgary, the Salvation Army, and several once-notorious old hotels: the King Edward, the St Louis, and the Cecil.

One could say that the discussion of Calgary's plans and ideas in this book culminates in the current program for the East Village. In it one can find traces of Mawson, Harold Hanen, and neighbourhood advocacy. It marks a turn away from unquestioned exurban development and will form a solid residential district paired with the east end of the Beltline, old Victoria Park, across the railway tracks. It is the new construction of an old inner-city neighbourhood, oxymoronic perhaps, but a powerful commitment to downtown urban living.

There have been several plans for this area. In 2001 city council approved the East Village project in theory, and in 2003 approved a planning program to amend the then current Area Redevelopment Plan. BKDI Architects, Lyons Venini and Associates, and Jenkins & Associates were the primary architectural consultants.

The area had been targeted for residential development since 1979 and re-approved in 1990. In 1994 some commercial development was added, and in 2001 the East Village Area Redevelopment Plan was made. The 2003 and 2005 amendments to that plan owe much to some of the suggestions in the 1912 Mawson Plan. All the Area Redevelopment Plans suggest roughly the same thing: livability, attractiveness, a good sense of neighbourhood, unique communities, diversity and variety, sustainability, and open spaces integrated with the larger park system — nothing anyone could object to. The differences appear in the actual proposed plans and their accompanying illustrations, which at an ARP level remain diagrammatic but also potent, dealing as they do with overall concepts.

2005 East Village Area Redevelopment Proposal

The 2005 East Village Area Redevelopment Proposal included 11,500 residents, plus commercial, service, and institutional uses. It was to be mainly pedestrian or bike-oriented, with cars downplayed. The homeless shelters and the senior citizens apartment buildings were to be integrated with sensitivity and understanding, and all in all it was to be a harmonious place to live. LEED® Silver should be the standard: water — storm and runoff — was to be managed throughout the area through wetlands, green roofs, and low-water landscaping. Brownfield sites were to be remediated and alternative energy to be investigated. Again, nothing to object to here, and these goals have continued through subsequent plans.

The urban design was built upon the history of liveable pedestrian streets, with examples directly drawn from Europe and older American cities. Parking was to be screened by buildings, and sidewalks were to have a sense of containment and community. The existing block pattern was to be maintained, only broken by the emergence of the northeast LRT line, curving through the area on its way to cross the Bow River. In general, the buildings create street walls, but the blocks themselves are permeable, with alleys and interior courts. Avenues connect to existing arteries, and 4th Street is a major roadway with an underpass (under the CPR tracks) to the Stampede Grounds.

Figure 43-3. The cover of the 2005 Area Redevelopment Plan: Calgary softened by watercolour, a soft summer afternoon, families, children, and couples strolling.

Land Use Planning & Policy, Planning Development & Assessment Department, The City of Calgary. East Village Area Redevelopment Plan, 2005.

A network of landmarks and vistas was proposed, and this is where the 2005 plan connects with Mawson's Calgary, the City Beautiful of 1912. The 2005 objective was to "define a series of civic landmarks and vistas that visually link public spaces, enhance wayfinding and create a sense of place."[1] These elements would be fountains, sculptures, and specially shaped buildings; view corridors were to be maintained to the Bow River, Fort Calgary, and the Saddledome. Such qualities and events are carefully mapped in this plan, the underlying belief being that there are formal rules that give order to a city, and in the absence of any existing social or built fabric, it is possible to invent a neighbourhood that will appear to be grounded in history. It might not be Calgary's history,

---

1 2005 Master Plan.

Figure 43-4. From the 2005 Area Redevelopment Plan. The top shows the reality, the bottom indicates a reinstatement of a 1910 Calgary, replicating a pre-modern sandstone-and-brick townscape.
Land Use Planning & Policy, Planning Development & Assessment Department, The City of Calgary. East Village Area Redevelopment Plan, 2005.

but that isn't a concern. Calgary needs a history — Mawson thought so ninety years earlier, and evidently in 2005, it was still looking.

The overall urbanity of the plan is dependent on the 11,500 people living in it, buying their food there, using its restaurants, its market, its outdoor living areas, walking to work, and if they must, using LRT connections to access the suburban city. This is a worldly concept, with cobbled paving and avenues lined with trees, shops, and entertainments on the ground floor with apartments above. It would be wonderful and completely unique in Calgary. Not a single-family house in sight.

In this 2005 plan, 8th Avenue East reinstates Harold Hanen's proposal for a reconstructed 8th Avenue of small shops, the old hotel: a little main street like the ones found in Calgary's inner-city neighbourhoods. A classical building is proposed for the back of the Municipal Building, providing a terminal axis at the west end of 8th Avenue, and shielding the almost nineteenth-century Parisian scale and architecture of this proposal from the looming cliff of early 1980s mirrored-glass modernity that forms the eastern edge of the downtown business core.

2007 RIVERS DISTRICT COMMUNITY REVITALIZATION PLAN

Just two years after the 2005 East Village Area Redevelopment Amendment, the Rivers District Community Revitalization Plan was released and adopted by city council. The Rivers District encompasses the entire west side of the Elbow River from the Bow to the south edge of the Stampede Grounds, where it abuts an up-river bend of the Elbow and is bounded by 1st Street Southeast on the west. As opposed to the Area Redevelopment Plan, this amendment outlines in great detail exactly what is going to happen on each plot of ground, how much it will cost, and how it will coordinate with larger objectives. We see that the East Village has been streamlined somewhat. Gone is the complexity of land use. The micro-zoning has been replaced by a coarser pattern. Ground floors are commercial throughout, with residential, commercial, or institutional uses above, except for a five-block residential southeast corner. However, the essential squares are still in place, as are the traffic connections.

In 2007 the Calgary Municipal Land Corporation (CMLC) was formed to strategize, structure, and create

Figure 43-5. From the 2007 Calgary Municipal Land Corporation Annual Report. Two years later, this same block, behind the Calgary Municipal Building, is not so prescriptive as found in the 2005 proposal. Instead, the shabby reality is fogged over, trees added, and much is left to the imagination. *CMLC Annual Report, 2007.*

opportunity in the Rivers District. This has moved the planning process out of the City of Calgary Planning Department into CMLC, a city-owned subsidiary in charge of the Rivers District Community Revitalization Plan. The drawings in the 2008 annual report of the CMLC, its first, are dramatically different from previous graphic presentations of the area. In this plan, photographs of the existing built environment are collaged with extremely ephemeral pencil and watercolour wash sketches — nothing too specific, no overly-determined architecture, just a feeling of casual, provisional occupation.

In 2008 CMLC organized an international competition for a new master plan for the redevelopment of East Village. The British architecture and planning firm, Broadway Malyan, was awarded the project. From Broadway Malyan's sketch of a possible East Village street life alone, one can see a shift in thinking: the sketch could be of any city where a modern commercial core has made provision for a public domain. The plan itself has cut a diagonal route through the old street grid, leading directly to the new St. Patrick's bridge. High-rise development is suggested on the old Marathon property between the tracks and 9th Avenue, giving the East Village a strong southern edge, while casting 9th Avenue into deep shadow throughout the winter. The LRT line, as in the 2005 plan, is flanked by some sort of shopping precinct. As a framework for future development, it is ordered without being regular, intense without being crowded.

As a response to the Broadway Malyan master plan, CMLC commissioned the 2009 East Village Opportunity (EVO), part of the East Village gateway zone, from Marshall Tittemore Architects. EVO was programmed as an identifiable landmark structure to act as an information and orientation centre in the short term and an open,

EAST VILLAGE PLANS   [219]

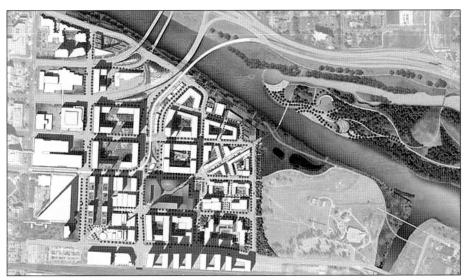

Figure 43-6. From the East Village Master Plan prepared by Broadway Malyan, London. More strolling; more people, more street life, clearly more leisure; no historic architecture, real or reconstructed, in sight.

BroadwayMalan. I Am East Village. Urban Regeneration, East Village, Calgary, December 2008.

Figure 43-7. East Village Master Plan. Clearly, from these two provocative images, Calgary has entered the brave world of British shapely buildings.

Marshall Tittemore Architects, Calgary, Alberta.

flexible community centre in the long term. It indicates something of the liberation inherent in the 2008 master plan that calls up such beautiful, inventive, sophisticated work, including the Riverwalk, the St. Patrick's footbridge, and future development of all the East Village land parcels.

East Village, Rivers District, Riverwalk

In 2010 CMLC and Stantec presented Riverwalk phase two concept drawings, and in 2011, a master plan for St. Patrick's Island. A bridge connecting the Riverwalk with St. Patrick's Island and the north bank of the Bow River and Bridgeland makes its appearance. In this document we are introduced to biophilic design, an opportunity, given the examples shown, for very metaphoric and poetic architecture, not commercial at all, structures that use rain and wind, plants and shade.

In just six years, we have moved from a historicist postmodern urbanism to an environmental architecture that references J.B. Jackson, Frank Gehry, Aeolian harps, tree houses, and boardwalks through wetland marshes. What happened? There has been a paradigm shift in design thinking in Calgary. Recovering a lost history is no longer the focus — the environment is. It is possible that mourning the absence of history while tearing down the historical is a thing of the past. Calgary has reached a critical mass whereby what it is, its current economic successes, its status as a cultural capital in Canada, has given

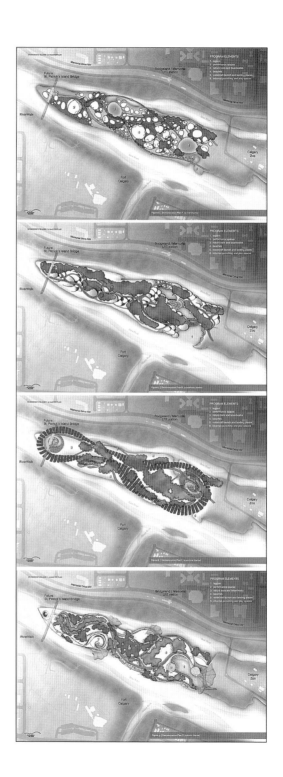

Figure 43-8. Prepared by Stantec and CMLC, St. Patrick's Island, A Master Plan, 2011. Demonstration projects, each emphasising aspects of the island: flora and fauna, archeology, geology, and leisure activities.
Stantec and CMLC. St. Patrick's Island, A Master Plan, 2011.

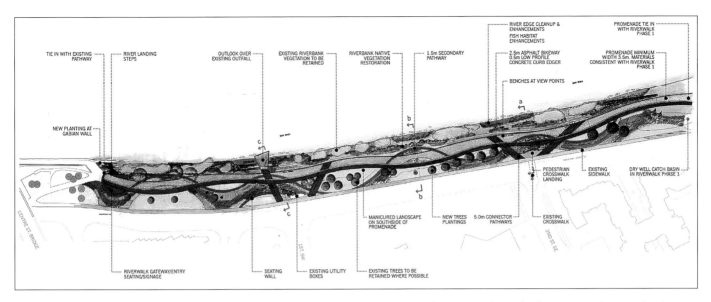

Figure 43-9. What a long way Calgary has come since the 1963 proposal to put the CPR tracks and a freeway on this riverbank.
Stantec and CMLC. Riverwalk Stage 1, Phase 2 Concept Plan, February 2010.

it the freedom to look outside itself and its own development history. Broadway Malyan, architects and planners not from Calgary, not from Alberta or even Canada, has seen Calgary in a very different way than anyone has in the past. Calgary is a wealthy energy head-office city in a beautiful location. It doesn't have many problems other than the opprobrium heaped upon it from Canadians who don't live in Calgary. If one lives here, and regularly travels to other large Canadian cities, one has to get used to hearing Calgary described in outstandingly inaccurate, misinformed, and deeply prejudicial terms. And yet, for people who travel the cities of oil, gas, and energy-production, Calgary is legitimately part of an urban discussion that includes London, Houston, Caracas, Riyadh, and places such as Khanty-Mansiysk in Siberia, a growing showcase of contemporary architecture.

Calgary has a context other than Canada. The beginning of construction in the East Village, such as the beautiful 4th Street East underpass by Marshall Tittemore, and the plans for parcels held by Embassy Bosa Developments (condo developers from Vancouver, originally from California) and FRAM+Slokker Developments (FRAM, an old Calgary real estate company, and Slokker Group from Amsterdam) indicate a globalization of Calgary's outlook, no longer homegrown and overly cautious, but more confident.

As we have seen throughout this history, there are not a lot of plans or projects that were ever allowed to develop too far if there was any hint they weren't going to be built. The pragmatic and conservative nature of Calgary does not allow it to spend a lot of money on schemes and dreams. And where a lot of money was spent, the much-debated Calatrava Peace Bridge for example, Calgarians have objected to the costs. Whatever civic hubris takes hold every so often during a boom, the citizens themselves are less keen on profligate spending; so many of them remember that all booms end in crashing recessions that can last for years. This acts as a natural brake on development. We must too remember that the development of the East Village, the reworking of the roads, the infrastructure, the putting of development packages in place, has all happened since the 2008 financial crash. Calgary has, through the nature of its energy resource base, been insulated from that shock. The housing market did not soar as high as that of Vancouver or Toronto, and it will not fall as far. This is the other side of conservatism, an inbuilt kind of caution.

We have shown a selection of unbuilt projects for Calgary, choosing those containing significant ideas that have carried on in the public imagination. Many of the issues that young architects were dealing with in the 1950s or the 1960s are still the issues that concern Calgary today. The phenomenon of the wheat boom at the beginning of the twentieth century had all the outlines of the oil boom of the 1970s, and these outlines are not unfamiliar to anyone in the energy boom of the 2010s. The ability of visiting planners such as Mawson to see potential and opportunity in Calgary in the early twentieth century is echoed in the number of external architects with global practices working in Calgary in the early twenty-first century.

Bibliography

Alberta in the 20th Century: the Great War and Its Consequences 1914–1920. Volume 4. Edmonton: United Western Communications, 1994.

Baine, Richard P. *Calgary: An Urban Study*. Toronto: Clarke, Irwin & Co, 1973.

Becker, Paula, and Alan J. Stein. *The Future Remembered: The 1962 Seattle World's Fair and Its Legacy*. Seattle: HistoryLink/HistoryInk and Seattle Center Foundation, 2011.

Cook, Walter. Review of Janet Waymark's *Thomas Mawson: Life, Gardens and Landscapes* (London: Frances Lincoln, 2009). Retrieved from *http://environmentalhistory-au-nz.oorg/2010/08/review-article-thomas-mawson-life-gardens-and-landscapes*.

Dempsey, Hugh, editor. *The CPR West: The Iron Road and the Making of a Nation*. Vancouver: Douglas & McIntyre, 1984.

Foran, Max. *Icon, Brand, Myth: The Calgary Stampede*. Edmonton: Athabasca University Press, 2008.

Francis, R. Douglas, and Howard Palmer, editors. *The Prairie West: Historical Readings*, 2nd edition. Edmonton: Pico Pica Press and the University of Alberta Press, 1992.

Grey, James Henry. *R.B. Bennett: The Calgary Years*. Toronto: University of Toronto Press, 1991.

Guimond, Pierre, and Brian Sinclair. *Calgary Architecture: The Boom Years, 1972–1982*. Calgary: Detselig Enterprises, 1984.

Hayes, Derek. *Historical Atlas of Canada*. Vancouver: Douglas & McIntyre, 2002.

Hedges, J.B. *The Federal Railway Land Subsidy Policy of Canada*. Cambridge: Harvard University Press, 1934.

Jacobs, Jane. *The Death and Life of Great American Cities*. New York: Random House, 1961.

Knowles, Grant. "Happy Valley: Early Beginnings and Modern History." *Valley Breeze*, December 2003.

Mawson, Thomas. *The City of Calgary Past, Present, and Future: A Preliminary Scheme for Controlling the Economic Growth of the City*. London: Thomas H. Mawson & Sons, 1912.

_____. *Civic Art: Studies in Town Planning, Parks, Boulevards and Open Spaces*. London: B T Batsford, 1911.

McInnis, Marvin. *Canadian Economic Development in the Wheat Boom Era: A Reassessment*. Department of Economics, Queen's University, *qed.econ.queensu.ca/faculty/mcinnis/Cdadevelopment1.pdf*.

Melnyk, Bryan. *Calgary Builds: The emergence of an urban landscape 1905–1914*. Regina: Alberta Culture and the Canadian Plains Research Centre, 1985.

Moran, S. "Surficial Geology of the Calgary Urban Area." *Alberta Geological Survey*. *www.ags.gov.ab.ca/publications/abstracts/BUL_053*.

Morrow, E. Joyce. *Calgary Many Years Hence: The Mawson Report in Perspective*. Calgary: City of Calgary/University of Calgary, 1979.

Nickle Art Museum. *Calgary Modern, 1947–1967*. Calgary: University of Calgary, 2000.

Peach, Jack. *The First Hundred Years*. Calgary: Calgary Chamber of Commerce, 1990.

Platts, R.E. *Where Polyethylene Pipe Challenges Metal for Slab Radiant Heating: Technical Paper No. 151 of the Division of Building Research*. Ottawa: National Research Council, 1963.

Prudential Toole Real Estate. "History," *www.prutup.com*.

Sandalack, Beverly, and Andrei Nicolai. *The Calgary Project: Urban Form/Urban Life*. Calgary: University of Calgary Press, 2006.

Sproule, Albert Preferick. *The Role of Patrick Burns in the Development of Western Canada*. Edmonton: University of Alberta Department of History, 1962.

Taylor, W.A. *Crown Lands: A History of Survey Systems*. Victoria: Registries and Titles Department, Ministry of Sustainable Resource Management, 1975.

Tomalty, Ray, and Murtaza Haider. *Housing Affordability and Smart Growth in Calgary: Final Report*. Sustainable City Program, The City of Calgary, 2008.

Tupper, Allan, and Roger Gibbons. *Government and Politics in Alberta*. Edmonton: University of Alberta, 1992.

Van Herk, Aritha. *Mavericks: An Incorrigible History of Alberta*. Toronto: Penguin/Viking, 2001.

_____. *Audacious and Adamant: The Story of Maverick Alberta*. Calgary and Toronto: The Glenbow Museum and Key Porter Books, 2007.

Walker, George A. "Canadian Pacific Land Grants" in Canadian Pacific General Publicity Department, editor. *Canadian Pacific Facts and Figures*. Montreal: Canadian Pacific Railway, 1937.

Wheeler, Robert F. "Organized Sport and Organized Labour: The Workers' Sports Movement." *Journal of Contemporary History*. Vol. 13, No. 2, April 1978.

Williams, Vicky. *Calgary Then and Now*. Vancouver: Bodima Books, 1978.

_____. "Settlement History of 'the Germans' in Calgary Between Ca. 1900 and 1914." *www.ualberta.ca/~german/PAA/Calgary1914.htm*.

Wilson, Michael C. *St. Patrick's Island: A Geological Perspective*. Calgary: FMA Heritage, 2010.

Archives

Alberta Provincial Archives
    W.G. Milne fonds

The Canadian Architectural Archives, University of Calgary
    Beatson & Finlayson fonds

Bibliography [225]

Chandler and Dale, Chandler Kennedy fonds
Cohos Evamy fonds
Gordon Atkins fonds
Hodgson and Bates fonds
Jack Long fonds
Ron Thom fonds
Rule Wynn Rule fonds
Stevenson Raines fonds

City of Calgary. Motion Passed by City Council at Special Meeting, January 22, 1964

City of Calgary Planning Department.
Canadian Pacific Railway Downtown Redevelopment Proposals, November 1963
The Downtown Pedestrian, March 1970
Future of Victoria Park, August 1971
Downtown Plan, September 1978
Potential Uses of the West Portion of Olympic Plaza, June 1985
Draft Reports of the Task Force on Housing in the Downtown: The East Village Planning Report and the East Village Marketing Study, May 1992
East Village Area Redevelopment Plan, March 2005
Rivers District, Community Revitalization Plan, 2007
Manchester Area Redevelopment Plan, 2008

City of Calgary Transportation. Transportation Infrastructure Investment Plan, 2009–2018

The Glenbow Museum Archives, Calgary, Alberta
Harold Hanen fonds
Molson Breweries (Calgary Brewing and Malting Company) fonds
Pat Burns fonds
Stanley Bates fonds

Private archives
Barry Johns Architect
Dan Jenkins Architect
David Lachapelle Architect
Gerald Forseth Architects
Manu Chugh Architects and Planners
Marshall Tittemore Architects and Planners
Rick Balbi Architect
Robert Ellsworthy Architect
Ron Boruk Architect
Saucier + Perrotte Architects
Saxby and Pokorny Architects
Tom Martin Consultants

Index

Numbers in italics refer to pictures and their captions.

Abugov and Sunderland, 93
Acadia, 188
Airdrie Airport, 123
Alaska-Yukon-Pacific Exhibition (1909), 36
Albert Dale & Associates, 34
Albert Park, 140
Alberta Gas Trunk Lines, *12*, 33
Alberta Railway and Irrigation Company, 25
Alberta 75 Place, *94*, *95*, 104
Alberta Transportation and Engineering Department, 83
Albertan, The, 30, 91
Algoma, 31
Allen, Bob, 127
Allied Works, 214
Alyth Yards, 71, 175
Anderson, Laurie, 14
Anderson Road, 153
Area Redevelopment Plans, 74, 190, 216, 217
Arnold, Arthur, *110*
Arts and Crafts Movement, 171
Arup, Ove, 83
ATCO, 120

Atkins, Gordon, 25, 26, *28*, *29*, 30, 34, 57–58, 65, 90, 96, *99*, 102, *118*, 150, 152, 153, *154*
Atlantic Avenue, *13*

Balaclava Heights, 135, 136
Balfour, 136
Ballyn, Christopher, 61
Banff Coach Road, 128, 131, 138
Bankview, 153
Barron Building, 91
Bassano Lake, 42, 159
Batistella's Colours, 191
Beatson Finlayson Architects, 27, 191, 193
Beaux-Arts, 45, 170
Belfast, 136
Bella Coola, 21
Belt Highway, 48, *49*
Beltline, 184, 199, 208, 215
Bentham, Jeremy, 43
béton brut, 27
Bighill Creek Formation, 143
Birmingham, 136
BKDI Architects, 215

Blackfoot, 82, 165
Blériot, André, 107
Blériot, Louis, 107
BMO Centre, *206*, 208
Board of Education building, 27, 90
Boeing, W.E., 36
Boer War, 22
Boruk, Ron, 184
Bow Building, 160
Bow River, 21, 24, 26, *29*, 34, 38, 42, *44*, 45, 55, 71, *72*, 75, 76, 81, 82, 89, 90, 97, 107, *108*, 112, 114, 116, *118*, 120, 124, 127, 128, 131, 143–44, *147*, 159, 160, 162, 166, *168*, 169, 175–76, 178, 199, 203, 205, 215, 216, 217, 220
Bow River flood plan, 89, 107, 118
Bow River Valley, 78, 116, 143, 150, 165
Bow River Water Council, *73*
Bow Trail, *138*
Bow Valley Ranch, 82
Bowmount Park, 146, 147
Bowness, 147
Brickburn, 116

Index [227]

Bridgeland, 144, *145*, 175, 190, 220
Britannia, 144
British Army, 21, 22
British Columbia, 17
British Commonwealth Air Training Plan, 123
Broadway Malyan, 65, 218, *219*, 221
Bruce Robinson Building, 93
Buffalo Stadium, 27, 31, 37, 71, 113
Burgener Lachapelle Architects, 95, 102, 104
Burnham, Daniel, 45
Burns, Pat, *20*, 82, 166, *167*, 172
Burns Building, 50, *52*, *53*, 166, 213
Burnsland, 138, 170
Burnsland Cemetery, *72*

Cairn Hill, 143
Calatrava, Santiago, 79
Calatrava Peace Bridge, 222
Calgary and District Agricultural Society, 199
Calgary Architecture: The Boom Years, 1972–1982, 102
Calgary Brewery, 27, 175
Calgary Centennial Planetarium, *122*
Calgary Centre for the Performing Arts, 50, *51*, 54, 55, 213, 214
Calgary College, 109
Calgary Drop-In Centre, 211, 215
Calgary Exhibition (*see* Calgary Stampede)
Calgary Flames, 199
Calgary General Hospital, 175
Calgary Herald, 50, 90, 91, 92, 93, 110, 127
Calgary Horticultural Society, 43
Calgary Industrial Exhibition Company (*see also* Inter-Western Pacific Exhibition Company), 199
Calgary International Airport, 57
Calgary Municipal Building, 54, *55*, 56, 60, 61, 63, 65, 67, 100, *101*, 215, 217, *218*
Calgary Municipal Lands Corporation (CMLC), 81, *218*, 220
lower income townhouse projects, 118
Calgary Normal School, 109
Calgary Olympic Park, 117, 118, 120, 124
Calgary Planetarium, 38
Calgary Police Station, 90
Calgary Public Building (Government of Canada building), 50
Calgary Public Library, 89, 90, *99*

Calgary Regional Planning Commission, 127
Calgary Sports Car Club, 123, 124
Calgary Stampede, *72*, 123, 127, *168*, 199, *200*, 201, 205, 208
Calgary Tourist and Convention Association, 123, *124*
Calgary Tower, 17, *32*, 34, 35, 36, 37, 38, 76, 160, *212*
other potential names for, 34
Calgary Transit, 57
Calgary's federal building project, 90
Camp Sarcee, 120, 128, *138*
Can Am series, 124
Canada Central Railway (CCR), *103*
Canada Life Assurance Company, 144
Canadian Architectural Archives, 25, 61, 67
Canadian Forces Base Currie Barracks, 76
Canadian National Railway (CNR), 23, 27, 58, 166, 175, *200*, 201, 205
Canadian Pacific (CP) Air, 23
Canadian Pacific Railway (CPR), 17, 19, 22, 23, 24, 25, 31, 35, 37, 38, 41, *44*, 57, 58, 60, 71, *74*, 76, 89, *99*, *103*, 136–37, 140, *167*, 169, 170, 172, 175
bridge, 82
engineers, 75
gardens, 19
Land Department map, *13*, 34
line, *12*, *29*, 58, 71, *74*, 127, 166, 175, 184, 199, 203, 214, 215
plan of downtown Calgary, 11, 76, *103*
service depot, *11*
station, 19, *20*, 22, *23*, 24, *28*, *32*, 43, *44*, 135
tracks, *13*, 42, 82, *118*, 170, 179, 216, 220
urbanism, 17
Cantos Music Foundation, 211, *212*, 213
Canyon Meadows, 153
Cardston, 25, 26
Cascade Development Corporation, 102
Catholic Separate Schools building, 27
Cecil Hotel, 213, 215
Cemetery Hill, *72*, *200*
Centennial Tower, 30, *33*, 34
Central Industrial Area, 170
Central Mortgage Housing Corporation (CMHC), 146, 194
Central Park, 93, 109
Central United Church, *49*

Centre Street, 17, 24, 35, 42, *44*, 55, 76, *77*, 78
Centre Street Bridge, 75, 76, *77*, 172
Chamber of Commerce, 30
Charleswood, 188
Chestermere Lake, 140
Chicago's Columbian Exposition, 45
Chinatown, *18*, 71, 89, 90
Chinook Arch, 160
Chinook Park, 188, 191
Christie, Ian, *18*
City Beautiful, 75, 171, 216
City Hall, 22, 27, 42, *51*, *53*, 55, 60, 63, 96, *99*, 100, 117, 201, 211, 214
City of Calgary, 24, 25, 26, 30, 33, 34, 50, 51, 67, 71, *74*, 76, 77, 79, 83, 89, 90, 93, 95, 102, 113, 114, 124, 127, *138*, 142, 148, *167*, 172, 187, 190, 194, *200*, 203, 218
City of Calgary Centennial Committee, 34
City of Calgary Past, Present, and Future: A Preliminary Scheme for Controlling the Economic Growth of the City, The, 75
Civic Centre, *44*, 50, *53*, 54, 55–56, 57, 58, 65, 100, 104
Claralta, 136
Cohos Evamy Architects, 128
Complexity and Contradiction in Architecture, 26
Connaught Estates, 184, 186
Convention Centre, 99
Cordilleran ice sheet, 143
Craigellachie, 22
Crescent Hills, *145*
Cross Streets, 48
Crowchild Trails, 97, *108*, 109, 115, 131, 165, 201
Currie Barracks, 120, 123–24, *138*, 188, 199, 201

Dale, Albert, 91, 97
Dale, Arthur, 57
Deerfoot Trail, 71, 165
Delmar, 136
Department of Public Works, *110*, *111*
Detail Plan Describing Arrangement of Workmens Area, Manchester District, 170
Dietze, Sigfried, *110*
Dominion Grid, *12*
Dominion Land Act, 137
Dominion Land Survey, 11, *13*, 17, 22, 75, 96, *138*, *167*
Dominion Lands Office, *12*

Dowling, R., 25
downtown core, 41–42, 55, 57–58, 76, 89–90, 93, 95, 96, *97*, 102, 107, 112, 120, 143–44, 165, 175, 176, 208, 211, *212*, 215, 217
Duany, Andrés, 76
Duck Lake, 22
Dunington-Grubb, Howard Burlingham, 109

East Lynne, 136
East Village, 55, 56, 57, 60, 183, 208, 211, 213, 214, 215, 218, *219*, 220, 222
East Village Area Redevelopment Plan (2005), 63, 65, 215, *216*, *217*, *219*
East Village Opportunity (EVO) (2009), 218
Eaton Centre (Toronto), *54*, 58
Eau Claire, 27, 75, 79, 120
Edgemont, 159
Edmonton, 21, 23, 58, 91, 109
Edmonton City Hall, 67
Edmonton Speedway, 124
Edmonton Trail, 97, 107, 147, 148, 159, 175
Edworthy Park, 42
Eichler, Joseph, 152
Eiffel Tower, 30, 31, 37
El Lissitzky, *122*
Elbow Drive, 165
Elbow River, 21, 22, 24, 42, 43, *72*, *73*, *74*, 75, 79, 82, 107, 143, 144, 165, 166, *168*, 175, 176, 199, *200*, 203, 208, 211, 215, 217
Elbow River Valley, 165
Elboya, 144
Erin Woods, 169
Esker Gallery, 178
EV Pedestrian Concept Design Study, 55

Fairmont, 60
First Avenue, 78
First Nations, 22, 205, *212*
First Nations highway, *73*
First World War, 31, 42, 45, 51, 75–76, 114, 137, *138*, 166
Fish Creek, 82, 140, 153
Fish Creek LRT bridge, 83, *84*
Fish Creek Provincial Park, 82, *154*
Fish Creek Valley, 82, 153
Foothills Hospital, 118, 120
Foran, Max, *200*, 201
Forseth, Gerald, 153, 190

Fort Calgary, 22, 24, 55, 79, 107, *138*, 201, 203, 211, *212*, 216
Fort MacLeod, 124, 170
Fraser River, 21
French, Lloyd, 191, 193

Gagliardi Group, 95
Gardiner Expressway, 24
Garrison Green, 120, 188
Garrison Woods, 120, 154, 188
General Motors, 31
Gerald Forseth Architects, 188
Gibbs Gage Architects, 160, 162
Glenbow, 58, *99*
Glenmore Reservoir, 166, 208
Government of Alberta, *111*
Government of Canada, 90
Grain Exchange, 22, 35
Grand Trunk Pacific Railway, *20*, 23, *108*, 136, *138*, 166, *167*, 203, 205
Great Depression, the, 45
Great Lakes, 21
Greenwich Village, 74, 174
Gresham Block, 178
Greyhound Bus Station, 57
Guelph, 95
Guggenheim Museum, 25
Guimond, Pierre, 102

Halifax, 21, 22, 67
Hanen, Harold, 50, 54, 56, 57, 58, 61, 65, *99*, 215, 217
Happy Valley, 123, 124, *125*, *126*, 127, 128
Harrison and Ponton's map, 137
Harrods, 22
Harry Hayes Building, 90
Hartley, James, *110*
Haysboro, 188
Henderson, H.A., *110*
Henri's, 178, 183, *184*
Heritage Park, 208
Highgate, 136
Hillhurst, 19, *147*, 176
Hodgson, Bates, and Beattie, 109
Holy Cross Hospital, 176
Homestead Act, *12*
Houston North, 90
Howe, C.D., 31

Hub Oil, *108*
Hudson Bay, *73*, 176
Hudson's Bay Company (HBC), 17, 22, 35, 42, *49*, 57, 58, 60, 99
Hull, William Roper, 82
Husky Oil, 34, 37, *58*
Husky Tower, 17, 24, *32*, 34, 37, 57
Hydrostone, 172

Imperial Oil refinery, 71
Inglewood, 19, 71, 175, 178, 214
Interstate Highway System, 22, 31, 36–37
Inter-Western Pacific Exhibition Company (*see also* Calgary Industrial Exhibition Company), 199
ISL Engineering and Land Services, 81

Jacobs, Jane, 74
James Short School site, 31
Jay Treaty (1974), 22
Jenkins, Dan, 120, *177*
Jenkins and Associates, 215
Jenkins Architecture, *177*
Johns, Barry, 121, 160
Johnson, Doug, 123
Jones and Kirkland, 61

Kananaskis Range, 165
Keith Construction development, 140
Kennedy, Chandler, 57, 58, 205
King, Madeleine, 190
King Edward Hotel ("King Eddy"), 211, *213*, 214, 215
Kinniburgh Slough, 140
Knox United, *32*

Lake Bonaventure, 140
Lake Bonavista, 140
Lake Calgary, 143
Lake Chesteremere, 142
Lake Ontario, 24
Lakeview Heights, 140, 188, 201
Lakeview Park, *141*
Langside, 136
Larue, Charles Eugene, *12*
Laurentide ice sheet, 143
Lenin Tribune tower, *122*
Leslie, Jack, 34

Life and Death of Great American Cities, The, 74
Lincoln Park Fields, 123, 124, 199
Lindsay Park, 58, *200*, 201, 203
Long, Jack, *122*
Lord Strathcona, 22
Lowes, Freddie, 144
Lowry's Gardens, 114
LRT, *55*, 57, 82, 83, *84*, 93, 97, 100, *101*, 102, 104, 153, 172, 176, 215, 216, 217, 218
Lutz, Ernie, 124, 127
Lynnview Ridge, 169
Lynnwood, 169
Lyons Venini and Associates, 215

MacCosham's, 203
MacDonald Bridge, 203
Mackenzie River, 21
Maclean's, 25
MacLeod Trail, 37, 65, 82, 153, 165, 166, 170, 172, 201, 203, *206*
Main Street, 55, 56
Manchester (Alberta), *12*, 172
Manchester Area Redevelopment Plan, 172, *173*, 174
Manitou Park, 135
Manning, E.C., *110*
Manu Chugh Architects, 81, *84*
Marathon Realty, 34, 57
Marathon Realty Tower (Marathon Tower), *44*, 97, 218
Marlborough, 191
Marshall Tittemore Architects, 218, 221
Martin, Tom, 83, *84*
Masonic Hall, 91
Mawson, Thomas, *12*, 43, *44*, 45, 75, 76, 107, *138*, *167*, 170–71, 172, 173, 174, *206*, 208, 215, 216, 217, 222
Mawson Plan, 43, 205, *206*, 208, 215, 216
McIntyre, Duncan, *103*
McIntyre Avenue, *13*, *103*
McIntyre Plaza, 95, 102, 104
McKenzie Towne, 56, 76, 154, 188
McVittie, A.W., *13*, *18*
Medicine Hat, 96
Memorial Drive, 26, 78, 81, 97, 116, 194
Meridian, 136
Mewata, 31, 38, *122*
Mewata Armouries, 113

Mewata Park, *115*
Mewata Stadium, 113
Milk River, 26
Millican Estates, 169
Milne, W.G. "Bill," *28*, 30, 31, *32*, *33*, 34, 36, 37, 46, 48, *49*, 93, 96, 97, *183*
Mission, 42, 175, 176, 177–78, 186, 188, 190
Mission Hill, 144
Mississauga City Hall, 61, 65, 67
modernism, *28*
Monarch Refinery, *108*
Montgomery, General (later Field Marshal) Bernard Law, 114
Montgomery (see also Shouldice Terrace), 114, 116, 120, 147
Montogomer and Bowness, *122*, 123
Montreal, 22, 60
Moriyama, Raymond, 50, 57, 58, 61, 65
Moriyama Civic Centre, *99*
Morley Reserve, 124, 131
Mormons, 25–26
Moses, Robert, 26, 71, 74
Mount Royal, 153, 175
Mount Royal College, 124, 201
Mulroney, Brian, 58

National Music Centre, 213, 214
New Edinburgh, 136
New Urbanism, 56, 76, 120, 153–54, 188
Nolli Map of Rome, 63
North Morley Trail, *108*
North West Territories Registration of Titles Ordinance, *13*
Northbury, 136
North-West Mounted Police (NWMP), 22
Northwest Territories, 22
Nose Creek, *108*
Nose Hill, *108*, 143, 155, 159
Notre Dame de la Paix Oblate Mission, 42
Nouvel, Jean, 214

Oblate Brothers, 144
Ogden, 169
Okanagan, 14
Old Calgary, 91, 92
Oldman River, *73*
Olmsted, Frederick Law, 45
Olympic Media Housing, 117

Olympic Plaza, 51, 55, 100, 117
OMA's Boompjes observation tower, *122*
On to Ottawa Trek (1935), 76

Pacific Aero Products, 36
Pacific Avenue, *13*
Pallesen, 135
Palliser Hotel, 22, *23*, 24, 34, 37, 43, 60, *97*
Palliser Square, 24, *32*
Palm Dairies, 178
Paskapoo Formation, 143
Paskapoo Slopes, 124, 128
Patrick, A.R., *110*
Pengrove, 194
Penny Lane Towers, 160
Performing Arts Centre, 14
Personnel Married Quarters (PMQ), 76, 120
PetroCan Building, 160, *161*
Petro-Chemical Buildings, 92
Petroleum Club, 57
Plaza Theatre, 176
Point, The, 176
Pokorny, Karl, 144
Prince's Island, 120, *212*
Progressive Conservatives, 58
Province of Alberta, 109, 123
Provincial Archives of Alberta, 30, *32*, 183
Provincial Institute of Technology and Art, 107, 109
Provincial Remand Centre and Courts, 90
Public Works Alberta, 110

Race City Speedway, 123
Ramsay, 153, 160, 203
Red Deer, 96, 166
Reform Party, 37, 58
Regal Terrace, 136
Regina, 17
Regina Riot, 76
Residential District, *18*
RFR, 79, 81
RFR bridge, 81
Richmond Road, *108*
Rick Balbi Architects, 148, 178, 183
Rideau Park, 144
Riel Rebellion (1885), 22
Riley Park, 176
Rivers District, 199, 205, 217, 218

Rivers District Community Revitalization Plan, 217, 218
River's Edge project, *44*, 120
River's Edge Village, 120
Riverside, 175
Riverwalk, 220
Robin Hood Flour Mills, 22
Robinson Hanson Report, 24
Rocky Mountains, 17, 121, 143, 159, 162
Romanesque Revival City Hall, 61
Ron Boruk Architects, 95, 104
Rosscarrock, 109, 112, 115, *138*
Rotterdam, *122*
Roundup Centre, 208
Rowan Williams Davies & Irwin, 95
Roxborough, 144
Rundle, 194

Saddledome, 38, 113, 117, 199, 205, *207*, 208, 216
Salvation Army Centre of Hope, *212*
San Francisco, 90, 152
Sandman Inns, 95
Sarcee Reserve, 128, 131, *138*, 166
Sarcee Trail, 128, 131
Saucier + Perrotte Architects, 213, 214
Saxby & Pokorny Architects, 144, *146*, 153
Scotia Centre, 58
Seattle, 36
Seattle Century 21 Exposition, 36
Seattle World's Fair, 36
Seattle's Space Needle, 30, 33, 34, 36, 37
Second World War, 22, 30, 36, 45, 76, 91, 109, 123, 165, 184, 201
Separate School Board, 90
Sevenoaks Apartments, 178
Shaganappi Golf Course, 184
Shaganappi Trail, 116
Shepard Airport, 124
Shouldice, James, 114
Shouldice Athletic Park, *118*, 120
Shouldice Terrace (*see also* Montgomery), 114, 115, 116, *138*
Silver Springs, 147
Sinclair, 136
Sinclair, Brian, 102
Singer, Hymie, 93
Smith Avenue, *13*
South Bow River Parkway, 74, 96

South Morley Trail, 108
South Saskatchewan River, *73*
Southern Alberta Institute of Technology, 176
Spanish Influenza, 76
Spruce Cliff, 114
Spruce Cliff apartments, 114, 184
St. Andrew's Heights, 144, *146*, *147*, 149, 153
St. George's, 136, *204*
St. George's Island, 120, *168*
St. Louis Hotel, *55*, 215
St. Mary River, 25–26
St. Patrick's Bridge, 79, *80*, 81, *84*, 218, 220
St. Patrick's Island, 79, 81, 120, *220*
Stantec, *220*
Stampede Casino, 205
Stampede Corral, 199
Stampede Grounds, 37, 58, 113, 117, *138*, 160, 166, 199, *200*, 201, 203, 205, *206*, 208, 211, 216, 217
Stampede Parade, 203, 211, *212*
Stephen Avenue, *13*, 51, 56
Stephens, George, *103*
Stoney Reserve, 124
Stratford Station, *101*
Sudbury Nickel, 24
Sun Oil, 92
Sunnyside, 175, 176
Sunshine Auto Court, 203, *204*, 205, *207*
Sykes, Rod, 34, 57, 89

Tipi Village, 205, 208
Tivoli Theatre, *177*
Tom Campbell's Hill, 144
Tom Martin Consultants, 83
Toronto, 90, 93
Toronto-Dominion Centre, 58
Townscape Properties, 118
Trafalgar Square, 76
Trans-Canada Highway, 22–23, 33, 36, 116, 117, *118*, 123, 124, 127, 128, 131
Trans-Canada Pipeline project, 31
trans-Canada railway, 42
Transportation Plan (1960), 24
Treaty 7, 82
Tregillis, W. J. 109
Tri-Media, 127
Tsuu T'ina Nation, 82, 159, 166
Turner Valley oil field, 91

Unbuilt Toronto, 67
University of Alberta in Calgary, 109, *110*, 112, 150
University of Calgary, 61, 107, 109, 112, *113*, 116, 118, 128, 203
    Faculty of Education, 109
    McMahon Stadium, 112–13, 117
urbanism, *27*, 28

Valley Ridge, 123, 127
Valleyfield, 169
Vancouver, 17, 21, 23, 36, 60, 76, 90, 222
    Food Action Plan (2003), 19
    Stanley Park, 82
Vancouver Island, 15
Varsity Heights, *138*
Venturi, Robert, 26
VIA Rail, *32*, 57–58
Victoria, 22, 67
Victoria Park, 190, 199, *200*, *202*, 211, 215
Victoria Park Exhibition Grounds, 205, *206*

Waterways Treaty (1909), 26
Wawa Goose, 24
Weadick, Guy, 199
Weaslehead, 166
Webb Zerafa Menkes Houdsen Partnership, 61, 102
Western Construction and Building, 91
Western Irrigation District, 140, 142
Western Union Building, *183*
Windsor Park, 144
Winnipeg, *13*, 17, 22, 23, 76, 184
Winnipeg Riot, 76
Winona Place, 136
Winter Cities Association, 50, 51
Winter Olympics (1988), 38, 116, 117, 121, 128, 160, 199
World's Fair (1962), 33, 36, 37, 45
Wright, Frank Lloyd, 152, *177*

YMCA, 90

Of Related Interest

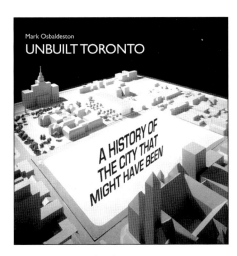

Unbuilt Toronto
A History of the City That Might Have Been
by Mark Osbaldeston
9781550028355
$26.99

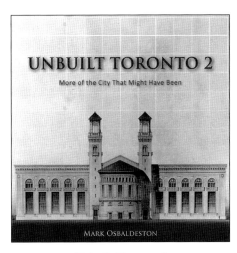

Unbuilt Toronto 2
More of the City That Might Have Been
by Mark Osbaldeston
9781554889754
$26.99

Unbuilt Toronto explores never-realized building projects in and around Toronto, from the city's founding to the twenty-first century. Delving into unfulfilled and largely forgotten visions for grand public buildings, landmark skyscrapers, highways, subways, and arts and recreation venues, it outlines such ambitious schemes as St. Alban's Cathedral, the Queen subway line and early city plans that would have resulted in a Paris-by-the-Lake

Readers may lament the loss of some projects (such as the Eaton's College Street tower), be thankful for the disappearance of others (a highway through the Annex), and marvel at the downtown that could have been (with underground roads and walkways in the sky).

Featuring 147 photographs and illustrations, many never before published, *Unbuilt Toronto* casts a different light on a city you thought you knew.

Quill & Quire cited *Unbuilt Toronto* as a book filled with "well-researched, often gripping tales of grand plans," while *Canadian Architect* said that it is "an impressively researched exploration of never-realized architectural and master-planning projects intended for the city." Now *Unbuilt Toronto 2* provides an all-new, fascinating return to the "Toronto that might have been."

Discover the scrapyard statue planned for University Avenue, the flapper-era "CN Tower" that led to a decade of litigation, and an electric light-rail transit network proposed in 1915. What would Toronto look like today if it had hosted the Olympics in 1996 or 1976? And what was the downtown expressway that Frederick Gardiner really wanted?

With over 150 photographs, maps, and illustrations, *Unbuilt Toronto 2* tracks the origins and fates of some of the city's most interesting planning, transit, and architectural "what-ifs."

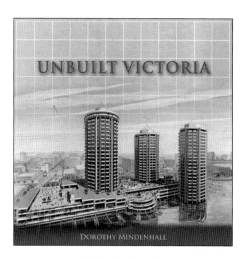

Unbuilt Victoria
by Dorothy Mindenhall
9781459701748
$28.99

For most people, resident and visitor alike, Victoria, British Columbia, is a time capsule of Victorian and Edwardian buildings. From a modest fur-trading post of the Hudson's Bay Company, it grew to be the province's major trading centre. Then the selection of Vancouver as the terminus of the transcontinental railway in the 1880s, followed by a smallpox epidemic that closed the port in the 1890s, resulted in decline.

Victoria succeeded in reinventing itself as a tourist destination, based on the concept of nostalgia for all things English, stunning scenery, and investment opportunities. In the modernizing boom after the Second World War, attempts were made to move the city's built environment into the mainstream, but the prospect of Victoria's becoming like any other North American city did not win public approval.

Unbuilt Victoria examines some of the architectural plans that were proposed but rejected. That some of them were ever dreamed of will probably amaze, that others never made it might well be a matter of regret.

Visit us at
Dundurn.com
Definingcanada.ca
@dundurnpress
Facebook.com/dundurnpress